COLLECTORS PRESS

Vintage Illustration

Discovering America's Calendar Artists 1900-1960

Vintage Illustration

Discovering America's Calendar Artists 1900-1960

Rick & Charlotte Martin

Collectors Press, Inc.
Portland, Oregon

A varying number of images contained herein were originally published by Brown & Bigelow, Inc; Osborne & Murphy Company; Osborne Company; American Art Works; Gerlach-Barklow Company; The American Colortype Company; Shaw-Barton Company; Kemper-Thomas Company and Thomas D. Murphy Company.

Sincere efforts have been made to include all names of publishers contained herein. In the case of omissions or errors, the publisher will gladly correct this in future editions.

Image Opposite Title Page: Fascinating, ca. 1925 by Gene Pressler

Published by: Collectors Press, Inc., P.O. Box 230986, Portland, OR 97281

Distributed by: P.E.I. International
Printed in Singapore

Editor: Gail Manchur
Editor: Michael Goldberg
Interior Design: Hoover H. Y. Li
Jacket Design: Patrick Prothe

First American Edition

10 9 8 7 6 5 4 3 2 1

Library of Congress Cataloging-in-Publication Data

Martin, Rick, 1963-
    Vintage illustration : discovering America's calendar artists,
  1900-1960 / Rick & Charlotte Martin. -- 1st. American ed.
        p.   cm.
      Includes index.
      ISBN 1-888054-00-X (alk. paper)
        1. Calendar art--United States--History--20th century.
    I. Martin, Charlotte, 1962-
  NC1002.C3M37   1997
  741.6'82'09730904—dc20
                                                            96-9529
                                                              CIP

Acknowledgements

This book was made possible only through the assistance of a number of people, unfortunately, they are too numerous to mention all by name. Our thanks go out to each and every one of you! Special thanks to Carol Schwartz and Chuck Kahle for pulling this information together and for all of their research and effort.

We have always believed in knowing where our strengths lie and knowing who possesses the strengths we lack. To that end, we would like to acknowledge and thank the following individuals for their invaluable contributions to this book:

Ben Stevens for the section on Rolf Armstrong

Carol Schwartz and Hugh Hetzer for the section on Hy Hintermeister

Robin Miller for the section on C. K. Van Nortwick

David Stick for the section on Frank Stick

Olga Steckler for the section on Bradshaw Crandell

A special thanks to the following individuals who contributed their time and knowledge to this project:

Terry & Margene Petros	Cary & Debbie Walmsley
Barry & Beth Mroczka	Rick Starets
Chuck Olson	Judith Bufkin
Sherri Biegel	Kim Kirkland
Jayne Hiebel	Jo Ann Havens Wright
Terresa Sandberg & Russ Salazar	Chris McCann
Fran Woodworth	Todd & Terry Riley
Ellen Riggins	Andrew Martin

A special thank you to J.I.I. Sales Promotion, Inc. of Coshocton, Ohio, for their assistance in researching the works of Shaw-Barton Company.

To all the people we could not list by name, our apologies and thanks for all of your help. This was certainly a community project. We hope you enjoy the results!

Dedication

This book is a tribute to the hundreds of calendar artists that may not have achieved the fame of their academic counterparts, but who, nevertheless, made a significant contribution to the art world with their gifts of beauty and timelessness.

Contents

8

The American Art Works, Salesman Calendar Sample, 1934

The Osborne Company, New York, 1906

Introduction

THE ART CALENDAR

Man has always recorded the passage of time. The first calendars were cut in stone and, through the centuries, time-keeping became more sophisticated. In the mid-to-late 1800s, businesses were distributing calendars to customers in an effort to generate customer goodwill. These calendars were very utilitarian and had none of the artwork we see on calendars today. The real beginning of calendar art came in the 1800s. During that century major advances in the field of printing occurred, including full color reproduction, offset lithography, and eventually photo-offset printing. By the late 1800s, reproductions of "Old World Masterpieces," such as DaVinci's "Mona Lisa," were placed on the calendars. Thus began the trend of using art on calendars which continues to this day.

These reproductions were readily available from art-print houses and were economically priced. In an attempt to differentiate themselves from the competition, and as a result of improved printing technology, they were replaced with original artwork by a number of modern-day illustrators. Calendar company representatives searched far and wide to locate

The Thomas D. Murphy Co., Salesman Calendar Sample, 1913

the most attractive pieces for use on their calendars. By the 1920s and 1930s, there were millions of calendars printed each year. Unfortunately, many customers received more than one calendar, so it was vitally important for businesses to insure that their calendar be the one used by the customer. To this end, buyers for calendar companies were required to keep a sharp eye on customer tastes and upcoming trends.

As technology advanced in the 1940s, color photography became the preferred image for use on calendars. As with most new advancements, it became more and more widely used. By the early 1950s, original artwork on art calendars had fallen out of favor. One of the major reasons for this was the high cost of producing calendars from original artwork. A photographic line could be produced at a fraction of the cost. However, original artwork was still used to supplement the photographic line.

THE BIRTH OF THE ART CALENDAR

Edmund B. Osborne and Thomas D. Murphy are credited with creating the first art calendar. In the late 1880s Osborne inherited a newspaper, *The Independent*, from his father-in-law. As a result he returned to his hometown of Red Oak, Iowa. He was joined in this new venture by a college friend, Thomas D. Murphy, who became half-owner.

A design contest for a new Montgomery County courthouse in Red Oak led to the creation of the art calendar. Osborne had an idea to print a photograph of the winning

design attached to a cardboard calendar, and then to sell advertising space around the margin to local businesses. The calendar was an instant success and the partners made a $300 profit. However, subsequent attempts to market similar calendars met with limited success so Osborne & Murphy went back to reporting the news.

The subject matter of this original artwork was largely determined by the tastes of the general public. For instance, the 1910s were dominated by scenes reflecting life in affluent families. The 1920s depicted art-deco and fantasy subjects. The 1930s had many scenes of Indian maidens and glamour girls, while "pin-up" art was the rage of the 1940s. However, through the years some subjects were perennial favorites: landscapes, children, animals, hunting, and fishing scenes seem to be found in every year's calendar line-up.

As calendar company owners and buyers became more aware of the desires of the general public, they would seek out an artist known for his adeptness with a particular subject. It was in a company's best interest to sign popular artists to "exclusive" contracts so the company would be able to control, to some extent, what art reached the market. As a result of these contracts, prints by a particular artist would show up only in those parts of the country represented by that calendar company. While some companies had a national presence, there were scores of smaller companies that had a strong following only in their region. As a result, the images that were most popular with the general public would be traded or sold between companies and reproduced as jigsaw puzzles, postcards, art prints suitable for framing, as books, or magazine covers. It seems some images were reproduced in every way imaginable! People developed a fondness for the calendar art hanging on their walls, and when the calendar was no longer useful they would cut off the calendar, save the artwork, and frame it so they could continue to enjoy it.

Osborne could not get the art calendar concept out of his mind, so in the early 1890s the partners agreed to enter the calendar sales business and formed a new venture known as the Osborne & Murphy Company. In the beginning, the company used illustrations in black and white half-tone. These illustrations consisted mainly of landscapes. After a few years the company switched from black and white to white with either green or brown. The choice of color was dependent upon what best

suited the image and it replaced the black ink previously used. The company added a number of salesmen in the first year and expanded its territory into other states. In the next few years the company grew rapidly. In the mid-1890s the partners agreed it was time to part company and pursue separate interests. Murphy sold his interest in the company to Osborne and agreed to stay out of the calendar business for five years. In exchange Murphy received the Red Oak *Independent* and a cash payment for the calendar business. In 1899, after substantial growth, The Osborne Company moved to Newark, New Jersey, to be closer to the art and business centers of the country. They soon expanded even further into New York City. In 1902 Osborne formed a new company based on a new printing process, later known as letterpress printing. The American Colortype Company was the first to successfully practice letterpress printing on a commercial basis. The

Brown & Bigelow, St. Paul, MN, 1937

Osborne Company was kept as a separate part of this new business. Over the years, the Osborne Company expanded internationally, and established plants in Toronto, Ontario, Canada; London, England; and Sydney, Australia.

Edmund Osborne passed away in 1917. The Osborne Company prospered under the leadership of William Seely for many years thereafter and acquired American Art Works of Coshocton, Ohio, in 1930. In 1940 American Art Works was again sold, this time to a group of former Brown & Bigelow executives headed by Jay S. Shaw of the Shaw-Barton Company. In the early 1950s, with outside sources obtaining a controlling interest in American Colortype Company, the Osborne Company was sold to rival Kemper-Thomas Company of Cincinnati, Ohio.

Murphy formed the Thomas D. Murphy Company in 1900 and built a new plant for both the calendar and the newspaper businesses. By the end of the next year Murphy's business had grown so large that he had to build a second factory. The Murphy Company was known for its use of advanced technology in printing full-color calendars, since Murphy was adept at perfecting the various printing processes of the time, and is credited with creating the first mounted calendar. The company was well-known for its attention to detail and use of the latest techniques. Even with today's technology, many believe it would be difficult to surpass the quality of this company's work. Like the Osborne Company, the Murphy Company also established plants overseas and created a branch in London,

The Gerlach-Barklow Company, Joliet, IL, 1912

England. This company focused on the smaller businesses and often sold calendars to local merchants in small towns. Murphy passed away in 1928; however, the Murphy Company continues to thrive today under its parent company, J.I.I. Sales Promotion, Inc.

The success of The Osborne Company and Thomas D. Murphy Company spawned the creation of a number of other calendar companies:

Kemper-Thomas Company: In the late 1880s Guido Kemper and Nick Thomas were salesmen for a large paper house in Cincinnati, Ohio. They started a side venture printing business advertising on paper bags. The company was successful with this concept and expanded to produce wrapping paper. This venture also proved successful and enabled it to expand to include other mediums, such as

cardboard fans and calendars. On the verge of true success, Thomas died unexpectedly. Ill health forced Kemper to sell the company in 1901 and he passed away a year later.

The company was sold to E. B. Danson and William Cooper Proctor. Danson was responsible for the day to day operations of the firm and he proved to be quite successful. Calendars were just one of the many things which this firm produced. It also specialized in cloth and leather goods for specialty advertising and is well known for its indoor/outdoor signs. The company is also credited for the creation of the first "safety calendar." The safety calendar was targeted at children and sought to teach them the rules of traffic safety. Subsequently, safety calendars became a staple of all calendar companies. Kemper-Thomas also developed the "franchise calendar" which was created for a specific

The Gerlach-Barklow Company, 12 Month Calendar Sample, 1932

industry, such as banks or grocers.

After World War II the company expanded yet again. This time it moved into specialty advertising on glass and ceramics. Kemper-Thomas had acquired the Osborne Company in the late 1950s and changed its name to Osborne-Kemper-Thomas, or O-K-T. It continued in operation until the late 1950s when it was acquired by Hallmark Cards of Kansas City. Hallmark Cards also acquired the Louis F. Dow calendar company which was based in Minneapolis. In the late 1970s Hallmark sold O-K-T to U.M.C. Industries of St. Louis, Missouri.

Brown & Bigelow: This company was founded in 1896 by a former Osborne & Murphy Company salesman, Herbert H. Bigelow, who was joined by Hiram Brown, a printer from St. Paul, Minnesota. Brown agreed to add much-needed capital if his name would appear first in the company name. He was not actively involved in running the business but did assist in acquiring artwork for use on calendars. Brown passed away in 1904 and in 1933 Bigelow died. Charles A. Ward, a long time employee of Brown & Bigelow, was named president of the firm. Under his leadership, Brown & Bigelow became the largest calendar company in the world.

Ward often signed successful artists to exclusive contracts and was instrumental in obtaining picture rights for the Dionne quintuplets. In 1932 he negotiated with the Boy Scout organization for exclusive rights to produce its calendars. The company also obtained an exclusive contract with the 4-H organization.

In addition to calendars, the company was also involved in novelty advertising. This field included metallic ashtrays, pens, personalized desk pads, desk thermometers, lighters, and leather goods, such as wallets. The company also achieved a great deal of success in playing cards. As card games were extremely popular with the general public in the 1930s, Brown & Bigelow created a program whereby its salesmen sold decks of playing cards and coupons to businesses. The coupons were distributed upon the sale of a preset number of goods with, for example, one coupon for every five pounds of flour purchased. This program proved highly successful for the company. Calendars were also offered as premiums. The Dionne quintuplet calendars were often distributed by businesses after a customer purchased a set number of products. Other very popular premiums in the late 1930s were the landscapes painted by Maxfield Parrish. In 1937 Brown & Bigelow paid $10,000 to Maxfield Parrish for "The Glen." Company salesmen were encouraged to use this information as proof of the cost-effectiveness of this calendar. For only the cost of a two-cent stamp, the business could mail this image to its customers. This premium was particularly popular with lumber companies.

Charles Ward successfully managed the company during the war years and served as president until his death in 1959 at the age of seventy-two. In 1959 Brown & Bigelow was acquired by Standard Packaging Company. Brown & Bigelow continues to thrive under its parent firm and today is one of the largest calendar companies in the country.

Gerlach-Barklow Company: The Gerlach-Barklow Company was founded in 1907 by two Osborne & Murphy Company salesmen, Theodore R. Gerlach and Edward J. Barklow. Headquartered in Joliet, Illinois, the company produced a large variety of calendars and often signed its artists to exclusive contracts. It also produced holiday greeting cards, fans, and direct-mail advertising pieces. The company gradually moved into leather goods and other advertising mediums such as pencils, yearbooks, and gifts. Like many other specialty advertisers, Gerlach-Barklow assisted in the war effort by producing canvas goods and patriotic posters. In 1959 the company merged with the Shaw-Barton Company of Coshocton, Ohio.

American Art Works: American Art Works of Coshocton, Ohio, was formed as a result of a business venture between two specialty advertisers named Jason Freemont Meek and Henry D. Beach. Meek began business in the mid-1870s as a newspaper publisher. To supplement his income he began to produce advertising items for local businesses. His first item was a schoolbook bag that was given away by a local shoe store, Cantwell Shoes. Within one year the advertising business was organized as a separate entity under the name of Tuscarora Advertising Company. In 1889 a rival newspaper man, Henry D. Beach, also opened a specialty advertising firm. The two gentlemen competed throughout the 1890s. In 1899 the two businesses merged and became known as The Beach Company. The company prospered until 1908 when it was sold and renamed American Art Works.

American Art Works continued to create calendars and tin signs. It is perhaps best known today for its tin Coca-Cola trays. Because of this company's success, Coshocton became known as the "birthplace of specialty advertising." In 1930 American Art Works became a division of the American Colortype Company of New Jersey. The calendar division was purchased in 1940 by the Shaw-Barton Company, which is now a part of J.I.I. Sales Promotion, Inc.

As evident by the number of companies created to market calendars, the art calendar was well-received by the general public. It soon became a popular method to promote a company's name and establish goodwill with its customers. Other major calendar companies from this period include Lutz & Gould, located in Burlington, Iowa; John Baumgarth Company, located in South Bend, Indiana; and Red Wing Advertising Company located in Red Wing, Minnesota. There were also a number of smaller calendar companies which served local customers.

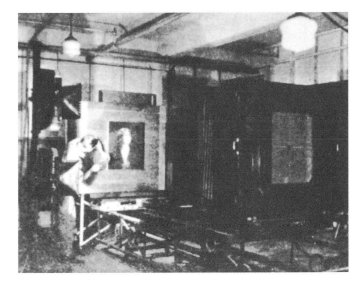

Original painting created from a live subject.

Photographing the original artwork.

Calendar Making Process

As described in the 1932 Gerlach-Barklow *Salesmen's Handbook*, the creation of a calendar from a work of art was an intricate and involved process:

The artwork was created by the artist and when complete, it was approved by a committee with years of successful experience in advertising art. Upon approval, it was taken to the photographic studio where it was photographed six times under bright lights, through color-separation lenses which would bring out every detail. Six glass negatives were then developed and retouched by a team of artists who worked at glass easels through which natural light was reflected.

The six negatives were then taken to the photo-composing room and were placed in a machine where, with the aid of a strong light, the impression on the negative was transferred to a sensitized metal plate. This process created a "positive" image, just as a photograph is a positive image of the film negative.

The positives were then taken to a proof press where one color at a time was added, beginning with yellow. Each plate was of only one color; therefore, six plates were necessary to create each print. The six colors were yellow, light blue, pink, gray, red, and dark blue. Each color was proofed and areas which needed correction were marked and returned to be etched to perfection. The metal plates were then transferred to press plates.

In the offset press room the thin, flexible press plate was attached to the metal cylinder of the offset press. Opposite the cylinder was a heavy rubber "blanket." The two cylinders were then pressed together and the image was transferred from the plate to the rubber blanket. The rubber then transferred the image to the paper run through the machine.

The giant press then produced large sheets of prints. The sheets were passed through the presses six times, once for each color. A typical print run consisted of 25,000 sheets, or a total of 150,000 impressions for each run! Each sheet contained twenty-one prints. They were then stacked in groups of 250 and cut to size, creating "mount prints," ready for use on calendars.

A committee determined the best way for the calendars to be matted and displayed. The prints were then sent to the job press department. Prints which were to be mounted were sent to a mounting machine where the work was done in a uniform and accurate manner.

The finishing department added the mats, top-sheets, ribbons, and other accessories to create a finished product. When pictures were printed as roll calendars, or "hangers," they were fed through a cylinder press where the advertising copy was applied. Those calendars were then taken to "tinning machines" where the metal ends were attached. At this point, the calendars were complete and ready to be shipped to the customer.

Companies amassed a large number of oil paintings as a result of the many years they spent buying original artwork.

Offset retouching the original artwork.

Photo composing machine.

Offset proofing.

Transferring the original onto the press plate.

Artogravure offset presses.

A lithographic offset press.

They disposed of these paintings by encouraging the salesmen to sell the paintings to their customers, sometimes at half of what was paid for them. A frame was generally included in the sale.

CALENDAR SIZES: Calendar prints were available in a variety of sizes, often ranging from 2 by 2.5 inches up to the "indoor billboard" size of 24 by 34 inches. They were also available in different layouts, with the images cropped to show different scenes.

THE CALENDAR ARTIST: The majority of artists discussed in this book are now published in book form for the first time, as they were not considered to be "real" artists during their lifetimes. This was largely due to the fact that they "worked" for a living, instead of creating art solely for art's sake. That is, the art they created was dictated by the wants and needs of the buyer rather than by the artist's "vision."

In the 1970s calendar art was rediscovered by the public and is now recognized and appreciated for its value. Today the reasons for collecting calendar art are as varied as the people collecting it. For instance, some collectors are interested in a particular subject matter, some in a particular artist, while others search for calendars from a particular town or company. All agree, however, that what was once considered the artist's "work" is now considered by many to be "art."

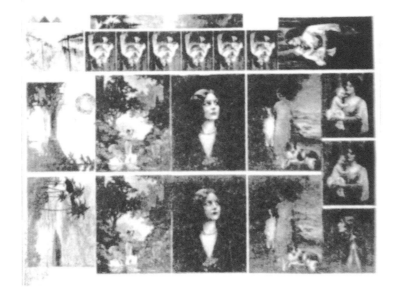

Press sheets.

Cutting machine.

Printing the customers advertisement on the calendar.

Market Review

Calendar art is becoming more and more popular with new collectors joining the ranks every day. While there are a number of reasons why people seek calendar art, a few trends have already emerged.

Pin-up and glamour girls are among the most desirable subjects sought by collectors, while landscapes seem to be the least popular subject. This may very well explain why Thompson prints are not as highly valued by collectors as those by Armstrong and Pressler. Because Thompson focused primarily on landscapes, his work does not have the diversity of the other artists discussed in this book. R. Atkinson Fox and Hy Hintermeister were among the most prolific of the calendar artists, as well as the most versatile. This versatility may well explain their vast volume of work.

Among the artists discussed in this book, some enjoy greater popularity than others; while some artists' works are skyrocketing in value, others are languishing at current levels. Understanding this is key to understanding the value of each artist's work. An example of work that is rapidly appreciating is the art of Phillip Goodwin. His work has enjoyed a substantial increase in popularity. When collectors believe that Goodwin's work has reached its plateau, many will turn to artists whose work is similar in style and context, such as Frank Stick. Another example of this trend is the increased popularity of Fox's work in the last ten years.

As Maxfield Parrish's work reached the height of its popularity and price, a number of collectors turned to Fox as a substitute.

Original art (not calendar prints) by these artists is also becoming more popular. A number of pieces have recently been offered at auction and are commanding higher and higher prices. The prices obtained vary greatly from artist to artist. A Zula Kenyon original sold recently at auction for $1,250 while a Phillip Goodwin original recently sold for $18,500. Original artwork by Arthur Elsley can command more than $10,000. Even with these examples of artwork commanding over $10,000, a number of illustrators' work can be obtained in the $300 to $5,000 range. The prices of original artwork are greatly influenced by the subject matter and condition of the piece, as well as the piece's origin.

Pricing: The prints shown in this book are assigned a price range which is dependent upon many factors, not the least of which are condition and size. These prices should be used only as a guide. They are in no way absolute. Furthermore, the prices quoted are for retail sales. Prints sold on a wholesale basis, or to a dealer, would command a fraction of the price listed, typically around 50 percent.

The "true" value of a print is what a buyer is willing to pay for it, or what price would satisfy the seller. Prints should not be bought solely as an investment because the market is a volatile one. The smart collector spends only what is affordable or comfortable.

Prices and images in this guide have been gathered from dealers and collectors across the country and reflect fair market values. Prices shown are for the image only; complete calendars and calendar samples, in mint condition, would add approximately 25 percent to the price shown.

Factors Affecting Value: An important factor affecting the value of calendars is the advertising that appears on them. The more desirable the advertising, the higher the price. Damage to a print such as fading, wrinkles, or tears detracts substantially from its desirability and decreases the price. Scarcity is another factor affecting the value of a print. Some prints seem to be in such an abundance that every collector owns one, while others are so rare that only a handful of them exist. Finally, prices will vary depending upon the region of the country in which the print is available for sale.

Reproductions: A downside to the increase in the popularity of calendar art is that reproductions have become much more prevalent. Amateur reproductions, created by using a color copier or similar method, are the easiest to identify. Professional reproductions have become increasingly difficult to identify. Unscrupulous dealers may go so far as to "age"

a reproduction. While there are a number of ways of aging a print, two of the more common ways are soaking the print in tea or coffee, or baking it in the oven to brown it.

When trying to determine whether a print is a reproduction, examine it closely and pay particular attention to damage to the print. Many times an old print with some damage is reproduced. In these instances you can examine the damage to determine if it is genuine or reproduced. Look especially at wrinkles and foxing (brown discoloration caused by mold). On the reproduced versions the wrinkles will be printed on and not have the "depth" of an actual wrinkle. Another method for determining whether a print is a reproduction is through the use of a jeweler's loop or high-powered magnifying glass. With experience, one can differentiate between the dot patterns of old and new prints. Because printing technology has evolved over the last hundred years, the dot patterns will vary between old and new prints. When using this method, focus especially on any foxing that appears on the print. In a reproduction, the foxing will contain a dot pattern because it is printed on; whereas on an old print, the foxing will appear as a brown stain.

While reproductions have their place in the market, to avoid buying one unknowingly it is best to buy from reputable dealers who are known and trusted.

The Artists

Untitled portrait, ca. 1928

Rolf Armstrong
(1889-1960)

Still considered today the undisputed "father" of glamour girls and pin-ups, Rolf Armstrong's influence shows in the work of every pin-up artist that came after him. Often imitated, his vision of female beauty and glamour is unparalleled in the pin-up calendar world. Armstrong painted in a highly personal style; it is easy to forget how stylized his work is. The beautiful faces of his women are too entrancing for one to notice the decorative treatments of everything else in his paintings. Even the artist's strokes in Armstrong's signature shows his sense of movement.

Armstrong was born John Scott Armstrong in Bay City, Michigan. Shortly after his birth, his family relocated to Detroit where Armstrong spent his early years. His constant sketching demonstrated his great aptitude for art and his family enrolled him at the Art Institute of Chicago. There he started using his nickname "Rolf." After graduation from the institute, Rolf moved to New York, with many other up-and-coming illustrators. His talents were quickly noticed and he was soon established as a popular and successful artist. His first calendar girl was published in 1919. Titled "Dream Girl," this print was extremely popular and was reproduced many times.

Successful, and now married, Armstrong traveled to Europe where he absorbed the atmosphere and continued to study and paint. He returned to New York in the early 1920s, opened a studio in Manhattan, and built a home on Long Island. It was during the 1920s that Armstrong completed some of his most famous paintings of beautiful, exotic women, including "The Enchantress," "Song of India," and "Cleopatra."

The next phase of Armstrong's illustrious career came in the mid-1930s when he moved to Hollywood, California. Here, the affluent Armstrong built a house and studio in Coldwater Canyon. His fame had already spread west and he soon befriended many of Hollywood's elite. This resulted in many commissions from actors and actresses as well as movie moguls and prominent citizens. For some unknown reason, Armstrong returned to New York in 1940 and took up residence in a fashionable hotel.

As the United States entered World War II, Armstrong signed a fifteen-year exclusive contract to produce calendar art with the Brown & Bigelow company. Pin-ups were becoming legitimate now and were considered a way to boost morale during the war years. Armstrong transformed his exotic maidens and Hollywood beauties into wholesome, but sexy, pin-up girls. He was fortunate to meet Miss Jewel Flowers, who became not only his main model, but the woman who rejuvenated Armstrong's career. Jewel's first pose entitled "How am I Doing?" was released in 1942 and became an instant success. This team of artist and model continued for many years and the prints featuring Jewel are some of Armstrong's best.

By the 1950s Armstrong was almost seventy years old, but he continued to paint and draw. He was fond of rural and western landscapes and beach scenes. He moved to Hawaii in 1959 and painted Hawaiian beauties on beaches. He died five months later on February 22, 1960.

Armstrong made strong use of lighting and many of his beauties are bathed in a characteristic golden glow of some offstage light or sunset. His use of pastels to create almost photographically smooth skin on his "subjects" faces is absolutely stunning. Whether depicting Salomes in gossamer robes or farm girls in dungarees, Armstrong women are timeless even though they are clothed in attire from different eras and distant fantasies. Armstrong was also one of the few artists who successfully produced almost full nude images, and that was because his paintings were considered art, not just pin-ups.

There is no doubt that Armstrong's artwork will command top prices in the future of calendar art collecting and his legions of admirers will continue to expand.

Yo- San, ca. 1929

The Eyes Have It, ca. 1928

Peaches, ca. 1930

Dreamy Eyes, ca. 1932

Sandra, ca. 1928

Foxy, ca. 1916

Norma Talmadge, ca. 1926

Dream Girl #1, ca. 1925

Dreaming, ca. 1930

Untitled portrait, ca. 1914

Forever Yours, ca. 1945

Charming, ca. 1940

Wonderful One, ca. 1949

Untitled portrait, ca. 1945

Hurry Back, ca. 1926

Here We Go, ca. 1950

It's a Date, ca. 1937

Song of India, ca. 1928

Hi Neighbor, ca. 1942

The Enchantress, ca. 1927

Kiss Me Again, ca. 1932

The Stewart Lever, ca. 1915

Let's Go, ca. 1946

Glamour Girl, ca. 1932

Encore, ca. 1942

How Am I Doing, ca. 1942

Orchid Girl, ca. 1926

Take Your Choice, ca. 1948

O Kay!, ca. 1938

Cherie, ca. 1954

Untitled portrait, ca. 1948

She's Tops, ca. 1961

June, ca. 1931

Radiant Youth, ca. 1938

Metropolitan "Drifting," ca. 1921

Beauty, ca. 1926

Thinking of You, ca. 1932

Untitled portrait, ca. 1928

Flower of the Orient, ca. 1932

Call Me Up Sometime, ca. 1939

Yankee Doodle Girl, ca. 1944

Lady Fair, ca. 1938

So Nice, ca. 1956

The Stewart Lever
"The Speed Limit," ca. 1913

Sunday Magazine, 1915

Dream Girl #2, ca. 1922

Cleopatra, ca. 1929

Hello Everybody, ca. 1930

Sitting Pretty, ca. 1956

Untitled portrait, ca. 1946

Let's Be Friends, ca. 1942

Haskell Coffin
(1878-1941)

William Haskell Coffin was born in Charleston, South Carolina. His family moved north and eventually settled in Washington, D.C., where Coffin would reside for the rest of his life.

Coffin's academic studies began at the Corcoran Art School in Washington where his obvious artistic skills quickly gained attention. Coffin's first exhibition picture was shown at the Cosmos Club in Washington and received an honorable mention. As Coffin's reputation grew, he traveled to New York where he received a scholarship at the Art Students' League. His work was also included in many exhibitions in New York. Coffin then traveled to Paris where he studied under Jean Paul Laurens at Atelier Julien. His work was shown at the Paris Salon, truly an accomplishment for any American at that time.

Coffin's production in the field of commercial art and illustration was enormous. He contributed to the war effort by illustrating posters and placards during World War I. In the 1920s and 1930s his illustrations graced the covers and insides of many popular magazines of the day, including *Cosmopolitan*, *Redbook*, and *Modern Priscilla*. Coffin was famous enough to be mentioned in an article from the *Sunday Star* (Washington D.C.), dated November 13, 1927. It featured a large photo of Coffin sketching a portrait of his wife, Frances Starr, a well-known actress of the time. Concurrently, many of Coffin's images were purchased by Thomas D. Murphy Company and Gerlach-Barklow Company, among others, to be used on calendars.

Haskell Coffin is best known for his pastel portraits of beautiful women. Some are bust portraits (from the chest up) but many are more complete portraits with the woman holding flowers, books, or a small dog. This type of portrait is more evident in his magazine covers. Many of his women radiate a haughty grace and evident aristocracy while sporting the bobbed hair and makeup of the era. Coffin believed, like his

contemporary Gene Pressler, that pastels gave a softer, more delicate effect than oils or watercolors. The daintily rouged faces and filmy clothes of his ladies bear out his artistic conviction.

Despite his artistic successes, Coffin's life ended on a tragic note. Plagued by financial woes and mental disabilities, Coffin committed suicide in 1941 by leaping from a window of the hospital where he was being treated for melancholia. He was sixty-three years old when he died, on the eve of World War II. We can only speculate on what work Coffin might have contributed to that war's morale effort.

The majority of Coffin's work found today is signed "Haskell Coffin." Many of the magazine covers and illustrations are readily available. His wartime posters and calendar prints are more scarce, and thus more valuable. Although his life ended tragically, Coffin's work endures as a testament to his talent and creativity.

Bonnie Mary, ca. 1929

Molly, ca. 1932

"The Prudential Girl," ca. 1918

Eileen Aroon, ca. 1935

Pansy, ca. 1923

Untitled portrait, ca. 1927

Rose O' My Heart, ca. 1910

Mother's Love, ca. 1927

Golden Hour, ca. 1931

Modern Priscilla, ca. 1926

Share in the Victory, ca. 1920

Modern Priscilla, ca. 1929

The Red Cross, ca. 1920

Crusader, ca. 1921

Untitled portrait, ca. 1927

Untitled portrait, ca. 1932

Untitled portrait, ca. 1928

Pride of the Farm, ca. 1927

Maid of the Mist, ca. 1932

The Lux Girl, ca. 1924

Untitled portrait, ca. 1935

Untitled portrait, ca. 1927

Vanity Fair, ca. 1910

Untitled portrait, ca. 1923

Joan of Arc, ca. 1920

Untitled portrait, ca. 1916

Untitled portrait, ca. 1927

Ruth, ca. 1910

Untitled portrait, ca. 1927

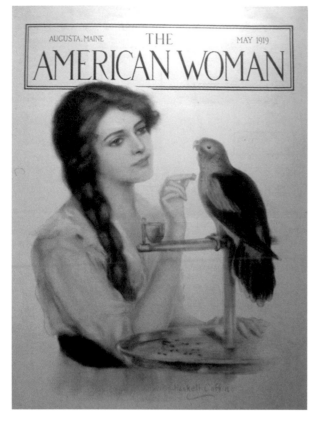

American Woman, ca. 1919

Sheet music cover
"Land of My Dreams," ca. 1922

A Warm Winter, ca. 1916

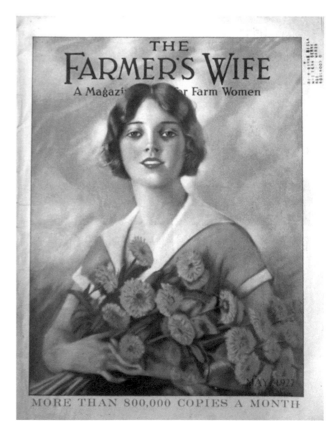

The Farmer's Wife, ca. 1923

American Magazine, ca. 1918

The Heart of the Rose, ca. 1924

Modern Priscilla, ca. 1925

Untitled portrait, ca. 1923

Untitled portrait, ca. 1923

Violets Bring Thoughts of You, ca. 1931

Arise, ca. 1924

Untitled portrait, ca. 1927

Peace, ca. 1921

M. Godovosky, ca. 1913

Untitled portrait, ca. 1918

Untitled portrait, ca. 1913

Josephine, ca. 1917

Untitled portrait, ca. 1924

John Bradshaw Crandell

(1896-1966)

John Bradshaw Crandell was born in Glen Falls, New York, in 1896. He studied at Wesleyan University and the Art Institute of Chicago. In 1921, at the age of twenty-five, Crandell's first published illustration appeared on the cover of *Judge* magazine. From the 1920s on his talents as a magazine cover artist were very much in demand. *The Saturday Evening Post*, *Ladies Home Journal*, *Colliers*, *Redbook*, and *Cosmopolitan* all featured Crandell art on their covers. Crandell also produced a series of cover illustrations for *Cosmopolitan* using Hollywood stars and starlets of the era. The popularity of this series earned him the nickname "The Cosmopolitan Man." During this time many of his paintings were used on calendars published by the Gerlach-Barklow Company among others. Crandell's artistic and financial success gave him the opportunity to set up a home and studio in New York City with his wife and daughter. He later joined the Illustrators Club and the Players Club.

In the 1950s Crandell stopped producing illustrations for magazines and publications and concentrated on portraits. He painted many state governors and other prominent society people. A feature article called "Where Are They Now?" in a 1965 *Newsweek* noted that Crandell, at sixty-eight, certainly profited from his successes. When not working in one of his studios on Long Island Sound or in Manhattan, he spent time traveling with his wife and, of course, painting. When asked about "the eclipse of the feminine form in calendars," he replied, "Today's dream girls are flesh and blood, not artist's conceptions." Crandell passed away in 1966.

Olga "Penny" Steckler, a former Crandell model, remembers portrait painting as Crandell's true passion. He saw his career as an illustrator as a means to an end. It provided him with the financial means to pursue his career in portraits. Ms. Steckler also recalls some of Crandell's methods. He worked almost exclusively from live models rather than photographs and would typically sketch the model and setting quickly. The finished work would be completed in three or four days! Crandell worked in either oils or pastels, depending upon his needs and desires at the time. Ms. Steckler humorously recalls that the parrot frequently found in many of Crandell's paintings was in reality a stuffed parrot obtained from a props shop. The parrot would be tied to the model's shoulder or propped up as necessary.

The bulk of Crandell's subjects, and particularly his pin-ups, are undeniably influenced by the Hollywood starlets. His early women depict maidens reminiscent of Lillian Gish, with their flowing tresses and sunbonnets and one-piece bathing dresses. Later prints feature shimmering hairstyles and sleek satin dresses of the 1920s and 1930s like those worn by Clara Bow or Jean Harlow. His prints of women with either parrots or dogs, set against stark black backgrounds, are particularly striking.

Crandell's style often seems derivative of many of his contemporaries. His use of pastels and his fascination with the starlet recall Gene Pressler's work. However, Crandell's brush stroke is a little freer and his style is more characteristic of traditional portraiture painting. These qualities do set his work apart from the other artists in the pin-up field. As more people recognize his individual style, his work is more popular and the value of his art has increased. However, much of his available work seems priced below other calendar artists of his time.

Roses of Romance, ca. 1931

Alluring, ca. 1928

Fine Feathers, ca. 1931

Say Please, ca. 1933

Untitled portrait, ca. 1932

Let's Be Friends, ca. 1932

Untitled portrait, ca. 1935

Accent On Youth, ca. 1940

Jerry, ca. 1922

The Bohemian Girl, ca. 1926

Untitled portrait, ca. 1921

The Sunshine Girl, ca. 1924

Untitled portrait, ca. 1936

Beloved, ca. 1937

Especially for You, ca. 1934

The Lady in Red, ca. 1933

A Dinner Date, ca. 1931

Untitled portrait, ca. 1916

The Gingham Girl, ca. 1932

Untitled portrait, ca. 1920

The Bathing Girl, ca. 1924

Smiling Through, ca. 1928

To Have and to Hold, ca. 1938

Mother's Favorites, ca. 1932

Untitled portrait, ca. 1922

Untitled portrait, ca. 1927

Untitled portrait, ca. 1922

A Mid-Summer Night's Dream, ca. 1932

Untitled portrait, ca. 1930

Untitled portrait, ca. 1934

Shirley, ca. 1931

Marilyn, ca. 1931

Faustine, ca. 1931

Patricia, ca. 1931

Eunice, ca. 1931

Gloria, ca. 1931

Alicia, ca. 1931

Jacqueline, ca. 1931

Arthur Elsley
(1861-1952)

Although not an American, Arthur Elsley's prints and calendars were equally as popular in the early 1900s as the American artists. He was born in London, England, in 1861. At the age of fourteen, he was enrolled in the South Kensington School of Art. His creative abilities won him a scholarship at the Royal Academy of Art two years later at the age of sixteen. He contributed paintings to Academy exhibitions from that time until 1908.

Having finished his schooling, Elsley started his career as art print painter in the 1880s by selling illustrations of animals for reproduction in black and white. Elsley's paintings of children and animals, which were very much in demand during this period, reached new heights in popularity. In 1893, a picture called "I'se Biggest" was so popular in England that a new copper printing plate had to be engraved because the first one wore out. From that time on, buyers were clamoring to obtain his work.

Because Elsley's artwork was in such demand in the early 1900s, it is odd that he commissioned only two pictures a year for American calendar companies. The Thomas D. Murphy Company used Elsley's pictures on its calendars between 1904 and 1924. The Osborne Company also used Elsley prints on its calendars. These two companies are apparently the only ones in America that bought rights to reproduce Elsley's work. His prints were among the most popular the companies produced.

During World War I, Elsley worked in a munitions factory where his keen eyesight and knowledge of metal work was put to good use.

A pre-1920s Osborne Company calendar catalog states " . . . there is no better than Elsley for portraying joyous, innocent childhood . . . always beautiful, always interesting, from the beginning of the year until the end." In the years after the war, his eyesight began to fail and he took up woodworking and carving frames.

Elsley's work best evokes the era through which he lived, namely the late Victorian era. Happy, affluent children in Victorian or Edwardian costume, and their pets, seem to make up the bulk of Elsley's work. The combination of children and animals and the sentimental situations in which they were set have rarely been more beautifully depicted than in the calendar paintings of Arthur Elsley. Among his subjects, paintings of little girls and Saint Bernards are possibly his best remembered pieces. Other subjects include children with ponies, kittens, puppies, and, in one print, "A Christmas Carol," a parrot! Elsley's mother and child paintings are also popular. The print entitled "Playtime," with mother, child, and kittens, illustrates this point.

Elsley's painting style gave Americans access to the artistic heritage of English painters. His landscape and walled garden settings are painted in a traditional, highly evocative style, in the tradition of nineteenth-century English painters from Turner to the Pre-Raphaelites. His children are timeless and their dress and hairstyles vary little through the years of the artist's output. The authenticity of this English artist has, no doubt, contributed heavily to his appeal.

Today, Elsley's appeal is just as strong. Because only two pictures a year were released in America, avid Elsley fanciers will have to search harder for foreign prints by this extraordinary artist.

Private and Confidential, ca. 1908

A Trial Trip, ca. 1921

Keeping Watch, ca. 1907

The Rescue Party, ca. 1909

Just for a Minute, ca. 1898

A Loyal Guardian, ca. 1926

Kiss and Be Friends, ca. 1901

Safe Across, ca. 1909

No Thoroughfare, ca. 1917

The First Swim, ca. 1906

You Dare!, ca. 1921

A Good Old Friend, ca. 1921

He Won't Hurt You, ca. 1907

Good-Bye, ca. 1894

Hide and Seek, ca. 1908

A Christmas Carol, ca. 1909

A Faithful Guardian, ca. 1908

Here He Comes, ca. 1917

Helpmates, ca. 1906

The Golden Hours, ca. 1906

Playtime, ca. 1893

Untitled, ca. 1896

Who Speaks First, ca. 1919

Forbidden Ground, ca. 1899

Which May I Keep, ca. 1902

Dead Heat, ca. 1903

Wait a Bit, ca. 1893

In Childhood's Happy Hour, ca. 1904

Robert Atkinson Fox

(1860-1935)

From the 1890s through 1935, R. Atkinson Fox was one of America's most prolific and talented calendar and art print illustrators. He was certainly one of the most popular. As the work of Maxfield Parrish moves financially out of reach of many collectors, Fox has quickly filled the void and become one of the more desirable artists for collectors. There are many Fox collectors across the country. There are also two collector clubs dedicated to his work: The Fox Hunt, run by C. Atkinson Fox; and the R. Atkinson Fox Society, an organization which holds an annual convention for Fox collectors, commonly known as "Fox hunters."

Fox was born in Toronto, Ontario, Canada, in 1860. He was the son of William Henry Fox and Sarah Atkinson. Fox studied at the Ontario Society for Artists and supplemented his schooling with travel and study in Europe. He began his career early as a portrait painter. His work was exhibited at the Ontario Society for Artists, the Royal Canadian Academy, and in exhibitions in major East Coast cities. To date, there have been almost 1,000 Fox prints positively identified. Fox moved to New York City and then on to Philadelphia in 1900. In 1903 Fox married and moved to New Jersey. As the family grew, so did his work as an illustrator for calendar publishers, printing, and picture framing companies. Fox was so successful and his work so profitable that he eventually moved the family to Chicago to be nearer one of his biggest clients, the John Baumgarth Company. Fox worked tirelessly until ill health forced him to stop. When Fox died in 1935 at the age of seventy-five, his calendar prints were as popular as ever. Fox prints continued to appear on calendars into the 1940s.

Fox was capable of painting almost anything the publishers and clients requested; and it seems he did! One of Fox's best remembered and most loved subjects included in his early "Parrish-esque" pieces depicted exotic gardens and dreamy maidens. His portraits of women in motor cars or women posing with a prize winning steer are more down to earth. While these subjects are less well known, Fox is remembered by many as a painter of cows and horses. Certainly he contributed his share of animal portraits, but his cow scenes (usually being herded or grazing) outnumber all other artists and he seems to have perfected the genre.

Another style that Fox hunters have found appealing are his rural landscapes and cottage gardens. The craze for cottage scenes reached its peak in the 1920s and Fox contributed some of the most captivating submissions to this genre. Fox also produced prints depicting children and animals, outdoor sport scenes, Indian maidens, historical scenes, sailing ships, and transportation.

Fox usually signed his work as R. A. Fox or R. Atkinson Fox. There were instances, however, when he used pseudonyms. He used R. Atkinson Fox when he fell under the spell of the Barbizon school of painting. He painted portraits of such notables as President Grover Cleveland and Princess Louise of England. Fox worked in oils from sketches, photos, and memory. Calendar companies wanted to appear as if they had a large number of artists working for them, so many artists also worked under pseudonyms. In later years, when Fox was displeased with the endless output of paintings demanded of him, he would sometimes sign a pseudonym to his pictures. A number of pseudonyms have been confirmed to be Fox. They include G. Blanchard Carr; J. Colvin; DeForest; Dupre; Elmer Lewis; Musson; George W. Turner; C. N. Wainwright; and George White. One name that is definitely not Fox's is the copyright of A. Fox. This copyright was first used in 1906 by the Joseph Hoover and Sons Company and is in no way related to R. A. Fox. This copyright has been found on calendars dating into the 1960s. Garnet Bancroft Fox (G. B. Fox) is another name that causes confusion among collectors. G. B. Fox was the nephew of R. A. Fox. G. B. achieved success as a calendar artist and cartoonist in his own right.

Brother Elk, ca. 1923

Northward Bound, ca. 1917

William F. Cody - Buffalo Bill, ca. 1912

Come Along My Beauty, ca. 1927

Contentment, ca. 1893

Toeing the Mark, ca. 1907

Our Country Cousin, ca. 1908

The Monarchs, ca. 1927

Supreme, ca. 1923

The Journey's End - Oregon, ca. 1915

The Bridal Veil Falls of Yosemite Valley, ca. 1911

Precious, ca. 1915

Me and Rex, ca. 1907

The Treasure Fleet, ca. 1925

Music of the Waters, ca. 1929

Romance Canyon, ca. 1928

Daughters of the Revolution, ca. 1900

Lenore, ca. 1906

Ready for a Cantor, ca. 1909

Old Pals, ca. 1913

The Barefoot Boy, ca. 1920

At Your Service, ca. 1912

Fraternally Yours, ca. 1932

Rest Haven, ca. 1924

The Mill and the Birches, ca. 1932

The Bridal Veil Falls, ca. 1911

Where Giants Wrought, ca. 1914

Garden Retreat, ca. 1927

Carefree, ca. 1922

The Magic Pool, ca. 1929

A Fallen Monarch, ca. 1923

Land of Dreams, ca. 1932

Clipper Ship, ca. 1922

An Efficient Guardian, ca. 1909

The Call, ca. 1912

Spirit of Adventure, ca. 1930

General Foch, Pershing and Haig, ca. 1920

English Garden, ca. 1924

Sunset Dreams, ca. 1928

Blue Lake, ca. 1926

Love's Paradise, ca. 1925

Cleopatra, ca. 1902

Enchanted Steps, ca. 1927

The Sentry, ca. 1932

Waiting for Their Master, ca. 1905

Pals, ca. 1915

Noble Protector, ca. 1918

Untitled, ca. 1919

The Best Pie Maker, ca. 1905

Holding an Investigation, ca. 1909

Prepared, ca. 1919

Old Rosebud, ca. 1914

Edge of Grand Canyon, ca. 1932

The Buffalo Hunt, ca. 1932

L. Goddard

L. Goddard was the pseudonym used by two artists, Mrs. L. G. Woolfenden and Rudolph Ingerle. They combined their talents to produce a series of idyllic images of motherhood, youth, and family life as well as many popular "Indian maiden" prints for calendars from the 1910s to the 1930s. The first Goddard print, entitled "The Last Swim of Summer," published in 1908, depicts two children taking a dip in the old swimming hole.

Mrs. Woolfenden specialized in photography, and in the early 1900s, advanced her career when she purchased the Arthur Studios of Detroit from the original owners. The Arthur Studios produced photographs of models and scenery for artists to use as studies for their paintings, as well as producing calendar images. Mrs. Woolfenden began to utilize a technique popular before the advent of color film: black and white photographs were hand-colored or "tinted" before being reproduced as color plates for illustration. Although her hand-colored photographs appeared on a few calendars in the 1900s, it was her collaboration with Ingerle that proved more successful.

Rudolph Ingerle (1879-1950) was born in Vienna, Austria. His work was frequently shown in galleries and museums in Chicago where he had studied at the Art Institute of Chicago. Some of Ingerle's early work can be found on calendars, but not as frequently as under the name of L. Goddard.

For their collaborative effort as L. Goddard, the two artists combined their technical and creative skills into a style that was unique and original. Mrs. Woolfenden took photographs of models in various poses. These were cut out, hand-colored, and applied to the canvas. Then Ingerle filled in the rest of the picture using oil paints since pastels and watercolor did not cover the photos sufficiently. Details were not only added to the clothing and foregrounds, but to the lush backgrounds as well, utilizing Ingerle's landscape skills. In the hands of a less professional artist, the combination of photos and paint to produce a complete image would often appear cheap and staged. Woolfenden and Ingerle, however, were able to merge these two mediums to produce art that is both believable and beautiful.

Many of the successful calendar pieces produced by the team centered around "maidens." Besides the popular "Indian maiden" prints to which Goddard contributed heavily, one can find maidens dressed in costume fantasies like pirates, Gypsies, colonial belles, and Salomes, with vivid and evocative settings painted by Ingerle. Among Goddard's well received subjects are women dressed in the fashions of the times, from the slight trappings of the fading Gibson Girl look of the 1900s, to the boyish look of the 1920s. During this time, the team produced a series of "goddess" prints featuring their photo-cum-paint women in wild, naturalistic settings compatible with their divine status. A good example is a print of Iris, the goddess of the rainbow, who is shown sitting on a rocky hillside with tumbling clouds and a rainbow behind her. The goddess paintings are simpler and more softly painted than other pieces of the time.

The L. Goddard team moved into a new phase in the late 1920s and early 1930s when the Gerlach-Barklow Company and Kemper-Thomas purchased several Goddard paintings for calendars. This new series portrayed a genre of increasing popularity at the time: the cult of motherhood and the family. Exceedingly sentimental and beautifully painted, these family images included portraits of mothers with infants; and scenes of families enjoying outdoor sports, gathered around living room activities, or posed outside of rustic cabins. During this time Goddard prints of women with horses or dogs, young couples in love, and Indian maidens were published by every major U.S. calendar company. The Goddard style also shifted. Although they still employed photographs, the artwork is less photographic and Ingerle's artistic qualities dominate the images, which result in a softer look.

The work of the two artists under the name L. Goddard should not be overlooked. The collaboration of two visual artists is a rarity in any genre. Woolfenden and Ingerle were able to combine their talents well, as their surviving prints prove. The sentimentality of their subjects is particularly appealing and should inspire more interest as time advances.

Let the Home Come First, ca. 1930

Home Is Where the Heart Is, ca. 1934

Just a Song at Twilight, ca. 1926

Where Love Abides, ca. 1934

Untitled, ca. 1932

Playmates From Shadowland, ca. 1931

Moonbeams, ca. 1924

Untitled, ca. 1927

Untitled, ca. 1923

'Neath the Tropic Moon, ca. 1933

Pandora, ca. 1928

Thiebe, ca. 1928

Flowers of the East, ca. 1925-1930

Diana, ca. 1928

Echo, ca. 1928

Untitled, ca. 1928

Garden of Golden Dreams, ca. 1926

Oh What a Pal Is Mother, ca. 1929

Supper Time, ca. 1932

Untitled, ca. 1934

Just a Cottage by a Waterfall, ca. 1927

Waiting for Daddy, ca. 1924

Out Where the West Begins, ca. 1928

Little Mother, ca. 1934

The Love That Only Mother Knows, ca. 1932

Spirit of Christmas, ca. 1910

Untitled, ca. 1922

Untitled, ca. 1916

Last Swim of the Season, ca. 1909

Daisies, ca. 1911

Pearl of India, ca. 1926

Untitled, ca. 1924

Waterlily, ca. 1928

Flora, ca. 1928

My Little Gypsy Sweetheart, ca. 1919

Penelope, ca. 1928

Blue Night, ca. 1928

Iris, ca. 1928

Ceres, ca. 1928

Golden Memories, ca. 1918

Untitled, ca. 1928

Untitled, ca. 1918

Untitled, ca. 1928

The Little Gray Home in the West, ca. 1933

Untitled, ca. 1928

Untitled, ca. 1931

A Fair Catch, ca. 1927

Phillip R. Goodwin

(1882-1935)

Phillip Goodwin was born in Norwich, Connecticut. He relocated to New York to study art and was exhibited at various prominent galleries of the time, including the Hammer, Latendorf, and Kennedy Galleries. Goodwin's first published work came in 1900, at the age of eighteen, for the *Colliers Weekly* Thanksgiving issue. In 1902 he left New York to study with Howard Pyle at Brandywine. He returned to New York in 1904 and began, in earnest, his great illustrating career.

Goodwin did magazine covers and illustration almost exclusively during the early years of his career. He illustrated Teddy Roosevelt's *African Game Trails* and Jack London's *Call of the Wild*. He also contributed to the field of advertising illustration. Brown & Bigelow, Thomas D. Murphy Company, and Gerlach-Barklow Company all used Goodwin prints on their calendars from the 1920s on. When Goodwin passed away in 1935, only a few landscapes and sketches by this marvelous artist were found at his estate. It was later found that most pieces were either sold or given away during the artist's lifetime.

Goodwin's specialty was without doubt outdoor sports scenes and hunting scenes. He is considered one of the masters in this genre and Goodwin fans are extremely avid fans. Goodwin traveled extensively to remote parts of the United States and Canada and became familiar with big game hunting, the life of the cowboy, and Indian culture. This prepared him to paint the scenes for which he became so famous. Goodwin also developed a friendship with Charles Russell, the great Western painter, and was a frequent visitor at Russell's Lazy KY ranch.

The influences of Russell and of Frederic Remington are evident in Goodwin's paintings. One can also detect the influence of the years spent under Howard Pyle, particularly in the use of dramatic scenes and figures in prints depicting logging, canoeing, and trapping. Prints like the "Cruisers" and "Taking the Trail" show definite influence from the Brandywine School.

The price of Goodwin's prints in the collectibles field average slightly higher than many others. This attests to his great popularity and the high quality of his artistic skills. His work is of the same caliber and his technique is similar to Frank Stick. In fact, the work of the two artists is often confused. Goodwin's work is more popular now, particularly with collectors of the outdoor scenes. This might be due to the many advertising illustrations Goodwin did for gun and ammunition companies during his career. Interest in his prints show no sign of abating.

Untitled, ca. 1906

The Dawn of a Perfect Day, ca. 1912

Untitled, ca. 1921

A Chance Shot, ca. 1913

Out Where the Skies Are Bluer, ca. 1911

Surprised, ca. 1929

A Successful Call, ca. 1916

Moose Hunting, ca. 1920

A Tense Moment, ca. 1933

A Break at Dawn, ca. 1914

A Northwoods King, ca. 1916

A Welcome Opportunity, ca. 1914

Untitled, ca. 1918

Unexpected Visitors, ca. 1918

We're Going Home, ca. 1914

Admiring His Nerve, ca. 1927

Untitled, ca. 1907

When Action Counts, ca. 1925

Untitled, ca. 1914

Bruin Survivors, ca. 1912

Who's Coming, ca. 1907

Untitled, ca. 1919

The Right of Way, ca. 1918

The Cruisers, ca. 1915

A Thrilling Moment, ca. 1931

A Steady Hand at the Helm, ca. 1911

Breaking the Jam, ca. 1915

Taking the Trail, ca. 1926

Untitled, ca. 1915

The End of the Day, ca. 1920

Untitled, ca. 1915

In Turbulent Water, ca. 1915

In Strange Waters, ca. 1913

A Challenge, ca. 1922

Where the Tall Pines Grow, ca. 1916

Blazing the Trail, ca. 1913

Cruisers Making a Portage, ca. 1915

Hewing the Way, ca. 1911

In God's Country, ca. 1931

Forest Ranger, ca. 1928

Untitled, ca. 1909

Untitled, ca. 1914

Time for Action, ca. 1918

Nearing the End, ca. 1907

The Refugees, ca. 1907

A Prize Catch, ca. 1918

Supper in Sight, ca. 1916

Reel Sport, ca. 1922

An Early Morning Thrill, ca. 1926

Adelaide Hiebel

(1886-date unknown)

Adelaide Hiebel (pronounced "hee-bul") was born in the small town of New Hope, Wisconsin, in 1886. Her family moved to the larger town of Waterloo in Wisconsin when Hiebel was very young. Her father, a prosperous tailor, owned a number of shops in the Waterloo area. Because of this, Hiebel became an expert seamstress, a talent she would later utilize in her rendition of fabric and clothing in her painting career. In some of her best pictures, one can almost feel the silky taffeta, the plushness of velvet, or the delicacy of the lace.

Sewing was not in Hiebel's future. At an early age it was apparent she had a gift for art. She liked to sketch and model figures out of clay. Her primary and secondary school teachers encouraged her to pursue an art career. For some reason she chose architecture and promptly took courses in the subject. Hiebel's health, always frail since childhood, prevented her from continuing her studies. Undaunted, she turned to fine arts. She attended classes at the Art Institute of Chicago, where she studied oils and sculpture under the supervision of a number of talented instructors. Her most successful medium was pastels in which she would create some of her more memorable works.

In 1919 Hiebel was an art instructor when she received some news from her friend and mentor, Zula Kenyon, an accomplished calendar artist of the times. The Gerlach-Barklow Company wanted Hiebel to come to Joliet, Illinois, to assist Kenyon in completing her work before health problems forced Kenyon to semi-retire to California. Hiebel went to Joliet, signed a contract, and successfully painted calendar prints for Gerlach-Barklow Company for the next thirty-five years. She was the perfect artist to fill Kenyon's shoes. The women were good friends and their styles were very similar. Hiebel spent the first twelve years working in a bungalow studio atop the Gerlach-Barklow Company building. Dissatisfied with those conditions, she eventually got permission to work at home. Between 1922 and 1954, the Gerlach-Barklow Company copyrighted over 250 pictures attributed to Hiebel, who was under exclusive contract to the company.

Hiebel produced beautiful results in both oils and pastels. Most of her earlier subjects were women. Many are highly romanticized, with the main concentration on the figures, whether bust portraits or full figure. Hiebel's women are not other-worldly, but refined and innocent. She also painted women with horses and dogs, a popular theme in calendar art, since the animal psychologically represented a surrogate male figure. Hiebel also excelled in other themes: mother with infants, infant portraits, and small children in cute situations. One such represented a small boy sitting in a toy plane atop a knoll with the caption "I wanna be a Lindy." Her children are sweetly sentimental and evocative of the different times in which she drew them. Hiebel also painted animal portraits (groups of puppies and kittens), landscapes, historical figures, and national landmarks. Undoubtedly many of these were used on postcards and as illustrations for history books.

Hiebel's art will always be overshadowed by Zula Kenyon's art. The influence is obvious and their styles are very similar; indeed, many people confuse one with the other. But Hiebel is a master in her own right. Some of her painting shows extremely photographic detail and her scope of subject matter is just as vast as Kenyon's. Her sentimental children are some of the best in this genre. Hiebel's art is gaining much interest and respect and climbing prices for original prints reflect this growing interest.

Sweet Baby O' Mine, ca. 1931

Who Say's I'm Out, ca. 1939

The Gobble-uns'll Get You, ca. 1942

I Should Worry, ca. 1932

The Temptress, ca. 1933

Welcoming the Bluebirds, ca. 1944

The Bluebird's Garden, ca. 1945

The Professor, ca. 1943

My Dixie Sweetheart, ca. 1934

Phyllis, ca. 1934

Sweet Girl of My Dreams, ca. 1927

Jessamine, ca. 1925

A Maiden Fair, ca. 1924

Bloom of Youth, ca. 1931

A Girl I Know, ca. 1925

Isabel, ca. 1928

Me and My Pal, ca. 1931

Those Endearing Young Charms, ca. 1923

Untitled portrait, ca. 1934

An Old Sweetheart of Mine, ca. 1931

Under the Southern Moon, ca. 1932

Pals, ca. 1923

Untitled portrait, ca. 1921

Cheerio!, ca. 1932

Chums, ca. 1934

Sweetheart of the Range, ca. 1941

How Dear to My Heart, ca. 1923

Vacation Days, ca. 1931

Moonlight and Roses, ca. 1929

Sunshine, ca. 1924

Washington's Childhood Home, ca. 1925

The Bluebirds Are Here Again, ca. 1932

Love's Fairest Flower, ca. 1930

Spanky's Safety School, ca. 1940

Safety Sue, ca. 1942

Stop!, Look!, Listen!, ca. 1943

When We Were a Couple of Kids, ca. 1928

I Wanna Be a Lindy, ca. 1930

The Traffic Cop, ca. 1935

Outward Sunshine, Inward Joy, ca. 1937

Daydreams of Summer, ca. 1937

Sweet Solitude, ca. 1922

In Dreamland, ca. 1938

The Buckaroo, ca. 1935

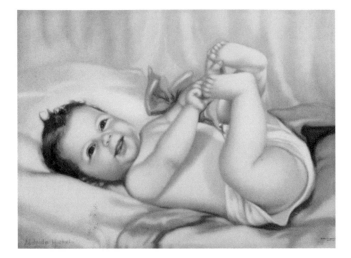

This Little Pig Went to Market, ca. 1934

Where Are You Going?, ca. 1936

Family Portrait, ca. 1937

Friendly Little Fellows, ca. 1935

Guardian of Yosemite, ca. 1930

Washington and His Birthplace, ca. 1922

Nature's Cathedral, ca. 1934

The Old Stone Bridge, ca. 1932

Be It Ever So Humble, ca. 1924

Hy Hintermeister
Father (1870-1945) Son (1897-1970)

Hy Hintermeister was actually a pseudonym for the father, John Henry Hintermeister (1870-1945) and his son, Henry Hintermeister (1897-1970), who created an abundant flow of calendar art and art prints for almost fifty years.

The elder Hintermeister, John, was born in Switzerland and received his art education at the Zurich Museum Art School. In 1892, at the age of twenty-two, he left Switzerland and came to America. Settling in Brooklyn, New York, he and his wife had a son, Henry, who would later become his father's partner. The younger Hintermeister studied at the Art Students' League of New York and eventually graduated from the Pratt Institute. Father and son worked closely through most of their careers.

In 1925 the Osborne Company commissioned John to create a series of annual calendars which related the story of American history from 1775 to 1787. The series proved extremely popular and was kept in production for over twenty years with both father and son contributing paintings. This started the flow of calendar paintings from the team which lasted almost forty years. John Hintermeister died in Brooklyn at the age of seventy-five. His son, Henry, died in 1970, in Pinellas, Florida.

The elder Hintermeister was an accomplished portrait painter who applied these skills to his calendar paintings. His early works exhibit a decidedly tighter, more traditional style of painting. His children and female subjects showed a very early 1900s influence. He also contributed his share of Salomes, hula girls, and bright young women, usually posed by a horse or motor car. The Hintermeisters' styles merged into a looser, more adept style as time progressed.

Like Norman Rockwell, the Hintermeisters excelled in the situational or storytelling illustration. This is usually a series that revolves around a specific subject, character, or group of characters. Possibly the

best remembered of these series are the "Gramps" series from the 1930s and the "Grandma" series from the 1950s. These portrayed seniors roller skating, playing baseball, and enjoying a whole host of "un-senior-like" activities with the neighborhood kids. Likewise, many of the Hintermeisters' outdoor sports scenes depict humorous situational events, such as a bear surprising the subject or fishing mishaps. Not all of the Hintermeister series were humorous. Straightforward depiction's include historical subjects, animal and child portraits, landscapes, and sailing ships. Their commercial commissions include covers for the *Country Gentlemen* magazine and advertisements for beer companies.

The art by Hy Hintermeister is the best deal today in the calendar art collecting world. The profusion of prints created by this incredible team should please any calendar collector and the wealth of subjects insures something for everyone's tastes. Hintermeister is far from undiscovered and has gained a large following in the calendar print world, and their value is rising.

Loose Ends, ca. 1953

Grandma's Tour, ca. 1967

Grandma's Tilting, ca. 1958

Catastrophe, ca. 1955

Cur-Tailed, ca. 1953

Hang On Gramp, ca. 1953

Atta Boy Gramp, ca. 1953

The Old Skipper's Pride, ca. 1938

Untitled, ca. 1934

Jes Swing It Nat' chel Sonny, ca. 1951

The First Bite, ca. 1952

Foiled by Br'er Rabbit, ca. 1937

Good Old Pal, ca. 1933

Two Pals, ca. 1932

You're Telling Me, ca. 1951

Traffic Tie Up, ca. 1948

Poppies, ca. 1937

Untitled portrait, ca. 1945

Alone, ca. 1935

Come On, ca. 1923

A Lady of Quality, ca. 1927

How to Land Them, ca. 1940

No Place Like Home, ca. 1949

The Happy Hearth, ca. 1948

The Timid Soul, ca. 1934

Grandma Takes a Ride, ca. 1955

Safety First, ca. 1944

Hold It, ca. 1939

The Last Match, ca. 1945

The Santa Maria, ca. 1938

Washington's Artillery Arrives, ca. 1943

Hello There, ca. 1923

Adale, ca. 1922

Chums, ca. 1933

Well Protected, ca. 1943

The Vikings, ca. 1938

Strong Interference, ca. 1947

The Double Catch, ca. 1949

Perilous Moment, ca. 1935

In Safe Hands, ca. 1941

You Will Become the Chief of Nations, 1938

Helen of Troy, ca. 1927

His Task Is Done, His Country Is Free, ca. 1943

The Bottom of the World, ca. 1931

The World Takes Wing, ca. 1934

Muson Arabian Stallion, ca. 1911

First Scent, ca. 1947

Precious Little Fellow, ca. 1932

Hey! For the Love of Mike, ca. 1938

Bee Ware, ca. 1944

Egyptian Splendor, ca. 1927

What a Pal, ca. 1947

Zula Kenyon
(1873-1947)

Of the relatively few women artists found in the field of calendar art, Zula Kenyon is probably the earliest, if not the most fondly remembered. The daughter of a minister, Kenyon was born in the small Midwest town of Deansville, Wisconsin. Although her talent as an artist was apparent from childhood, she was mainly self-taught. Women at that time were not encouraged to pursue careers, so it was probably with much persistence that Kenyon's family permitted her to travel to Chicago to attend the Art Institute of Chicago.

From approximately 1900 to 1918, Kenyon lived in Chicago. There she produced over 250 calendar pieces for the Gerlach-Barklow Company. The Joliet, Illinois, *Evening Herald* of October 29, 1914, carried a long article about the successes of the Gerlach-Barklow calendars and it featured a photograph of Zula Kenyon under the heading "Zula Kenyon of Gerlach-Barklow Ranks High Among Painters. . ." She is shown in the photograph posing next to a large urn while holding a bouquet of flowers, a romantic image evocative of lovely maidens of the times. She appears to be as attractive as the women she painted.

During the years in Chicago, Kenyon maintained a studio in Waterloo, Wisconsin, where she met another woman artist, Adelaide Hiebel. With similar backgrounds and interests the two became friends. Almost fifteen years her junior, Hiebel would soon prove to be an important part of Kenyon's career. When Kenyon became ill in 1918 and was advised to move to a warmer climate, she introduced Mr. Gerlach (of Gerlach-Barklow) to Hiebel. In 1919, when Hiebel was offered a contract to paint for Gerlach-Barklow, she moved to Joliet and took over the work that Zula Kenyon had started. That year Kenyon moved to San Diego, California. She continued to produce paintings for Gerlach-Barklow, but not at the rate she did previously. A few years later her sister, Hadiee, who was also an artist, joined her there. Not much is known about Kenyon's life or career after that. An article in a 1934 San Diego newspaper featured a photograph and story about the elaborate gardens the sisters had designed for their home. It also mentions that "Miss Zula Kenyon is a calendar specialist whose pictures many people undoubtedly have among their keepsakes."

Zula Kenyon worked in many mediums with ease, but her favorite was pastels. Dissatisfied with the materials available, she preferred to create her own. She ground her own pastel colors and made her own canvases and this gave her pastels the strength and brilliancy of oils. Most of Kenyon's subjects were painted before the 1920s. Many of her female portraits show trappings of the late Victorian era and a few, such as Lavinia, recall Sarah Bernhardt's stage characters. Other themes popular at the time included women in rustic settings, children, a "bluebird" series, animals, landscapes, and historical subjects.

Zula Kenyon was one of the most popular artists of her time and was well known for her richness of color, perfection in drawing, and beauty of composition. Her work is increasingly in demand by collectors of this genre.

In the Land of Dreams, ca. 1926

A Romany Maid, ca. 1932

Chrysanthemums, ca. 1913

Flowers of Autumn, ca. 1911

Memories, ca. 1924

Iris, ca. 1926

The Age of Innocence, ca. 1929

Untitled portrait, ca. 1918

Carmel by the Sea, ca. 1924

In the Heart of a Rose, ca. 1924

Lavinia, ca. 1922

Smiling Through, ca. 1929

Apple Blossoms, ca. 1917

Sweetheart, ca. 1927

Orchids, ca. 1915

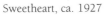

Untitled portrait, ca. 1911

Untitled portrait, ca. 1921

Glories of Life's Eventide, ca. 1930

Vivian, ca. 1913

The Springtime of Life, ca. 1912

Kentucky Beauties, ca. 1924

The Rose Queens, ca. 1915

The Sisters, ca. 1916

Dream Land, ca. 1922

A Gift From Heaven, ca. 1911

Her Favorite, ca. 1912

Kentucky Belles, ca. 1924

Nature's Shrine, ca. 1924

Love's Sweet Song, ca. 1914

Vanity Fair, ca. 1923

The Song of the Bluebird, ca. 1924

My Bluebird, ca. 1929

The Bluebird of Happiness, ca. 1926

A World of Happiness, ca. 1927

The Barefoot Boy, ca. 1914

Safely Guarded, ca. 1918

In the Land of Bluegrass, ca. 1925

Half-Dome, Yosemite, ca. 1920

Untitled, ca. 1920

Pride of Old Kentucky, ca. 1907

The Spirit of America, ca. 1924

Cantaloupe and Plums, ca. 1915

The Nest, ca. 1913

Fairest Flowers, ca. 1914

Where the West Wind Blows, ca. 1922

In Old Kentucky, ca. 1926

Untitled, ca. 1915

The Gem of the Rockies, ca. 1925

The End of a Perfect Day, ca. 1915

Gene Pressler

(1894-1933)

Gene Pressler was born in Jersey City, New Jersey, in 1894. The little information found on Pressler's background and early career merely states that he was a commercial artist and illustrator who specialized in chalk pastels and lighting effects.

Pressler's body of work consisted primarily of artwork for calendars and jigsaw puzzles, a genre that reached its peak in the 1930s. He is best remembered for his commercial art illustrations. Perhaps the most well-known was his work done for the Pompeian Beauty Cream ads, including yard long prints, from 1922 to 1926. Other illustrators who worked for Pompeian were Rolf Armstrong and Earl Christy, whose styles should not be confused with Pressler's.

To compete with Maxfield Parrish's series of calendar prints for General Electric's Edison Mazda light bulbs, Westinghouse Electric Company commissioned Pressler to design a similar series for its version of the Mazda light bulb. Whether his series compared well to the Parrish series is not known as Parrish's Mazda calendars usually take center stage.

Pressler was at the height of his popularity when he was struck down by pneumonia and died at the young age of thirty-nine in 1933. He left a wife, son, and daughter in Milburn, New Jersey.

Gene Pressler's calendar prints set him apart from other artists of the time. His women, more evocative than provocative, seem inspired by the stars and fashions of the silent screen era. You can see innocent Mary Pickford and Pola Negri sweethearts in sumptuously detailed attire. Another theme that reoccurs in Pressler's works are women with beautifully colored Spanish shawls. Some of these pin-ups depict typically American women draped in shawls while others show more exotic-looking females leaning out of windows and balconies in some imaginary Spanish setting. Pressler's use of pastels allowed him to add shimmering details to the dresses and shawls in his paintings.

Possibly the most stunning aspect of Pressler's prints are his lighting effects. Many of his prints featured light originating beyond the scenic borders or cast by a lantern or light somewhere in the picture. The reflective effect of the golden-orange light on the beautiful figures and their surroundings can be best appreciated by viewing this extraordinary artist's work first-hand.

Gene Pressler's work has already gained wide attention; his Spanish shawl pin-up girl (usually accompanied by a parrot) is probably the most recognizable. In his brief career, ended by his untimely death, Pressler created an astonishingly personal style of female beauty that is rapidly gaining an appreciative group of collectors today.

Untitled portrait, ca. 1921

Untitled portrait, ca. 1920

Someone Cares, ca. 1922

Fascinating #1, ca. 1925

Love and Kisses ca. 1922

Winsome Lass, ca. 1925

Moonlight and You, ca. 1926

Untitled portrait, ca. 1923

Unmatched, ca. 1927

Untitled portrait, ca. 1929

Untitled portrait, ca. 1928

Untitled portrait, ca. 1924

Untitled portrait, ca. 1922

Untitled portrait, ca. 1928

Sitting Pretty, ca. 1921

Seashore Romance, ca. 1930

Untitled portrait, ca. 1928

Jewels, ca. 1924

Enchanting, ca. 1932

Untitled portrait, ca. 1923

Daughter of the Nile, ca. 1931

Before the Minuet, ca. 1925

Inspiration, ca. 1919

Pets, ca. 1924

True Friendship, ca. 1926

Untitled portrait, ca. 1925

Fascinating #2, ca. 1925

Flirtation, ca. 1921

Untitled portrait, ca. 1926

Lucille, ca. 1926

A Girl of Long Ago, ca. 1922

Colleen, ca. 1932

Untitled Portrait, ca. 1925

The Debutante, ca. 1922

Say It With Flowers, ca. 1933

Miss Glory, ca. 1932

Thoughts of the Future, ca. 1924

Mothers Darling, ca. 1918

Untitled portrait, ca. 1930

Her Pride, ca. 1926

Untitled portrait, ca. 1929

Untitled portrait, ca. 1932

Carmenita, ca. 1930

After the Party, ca. 1927

Good Fortune, ca. 1925

The Old Oaken Bucket, ca. 1924

Untitled portrait, ca. 1932

God's Greatest Gift, ca. 1928

Untitled portrait, ca. 1930

Untitled portrait, ca. 1922

Untitled portrait, ca. 1932

Frank Stick

(1884-1966)

Frank Stick was born in 1884 in the town of Huron, in the Dakota Territories. His father was a banker and his mother had moved west from her hometown in New York state. In the early 1890s, before Frank was ten years old, his family moved to Sioux City, Iowa. Frank often accompanied his father, an avid hunter and fisherman, on many of his expeditions. This time spent in the wilderness had a great effect on Frank in his formative years.

In 1904, at the age of twenty, Stick moved to Chicago to enroll at the Art Institute of Chicago. Apparently his artistic skills were already well developed because, within four months of his enrollment, Stick sold his first painting. This encouraged him to seriously pursue a career in art. With the support of his instructors at the institute, Stick decided to move to the east coast to apply to Howard Pyle as a student. Pyle, an accomplished illustrator, was well connected in art circles and generally recognized as the founder and champion of the Brandywine Movement in painting. Other artists who would be drawn to this movement included Maxfield Parrish, N. C. Wyeth, and Jesse Wilcox Smith.

In 1905, Pyle accepted Stick as a student and the following year Stick moved to Wilmington, Delaware, to begin his studies under Pyle. Although not as rugged as the wilderness settings of his childhood, the beautiful Brandywine County with its deep forests, rolling hills, and many rivers, must have given Stick much inspiration. Stick supplemented his income by writing articles and short stories for outdoor magazines. Because of his love for outdoor sports, he concentrated most of his painting on this theme. He contributed many outdoor and sporting illustrations to *Saint Nicholas Magazine* during his training, as well as later during his burgeoning career. In 1909 Stick completed his studies with Pyle and left Brandywine to return to the Midwest. He and his family moved about: from a rustic home in the wilderness, to Chicago, and finally back to the east coast and New York City, which offered the greatest opportunity for Stick's work. By this time, Stick's paintings of outdoor life were very much in demand. For the next twenty years he would produce an immense amount of work for calendars and art prints.

By 1929 Frank Stick became disillusioned with his role in the art world. Although highly successful, he felt his true artistic talents were being trivialized for commercial needs; so he discontinued working as a commercial illustrator. He vowed never to paint commercially again, but to paint only for his personal satisfaction. Over the years, Stick became involved in many civic projects. In the 1920s he became mayor of Interlaken, New York. His love of the outdoors led him to be active in a number of conservation groups, including the Izaak Walton League. In 1981, thirteen years after his death at the age of eighty-two, *An Artist's Catch* was published. This book features Stick's 300 beautiful watercolors of fresh and saltwater fish.

Frank Stick's outdoor sports illustrations constitute a genre unto themselves. The theme is usually one of man and nature. Most of his scenes depict hunters (with or without dogs), fishermen, or hunting and camping expeditions. The landscape of these scenes, whether fields or mountains, demands attention. Stick also did a series of beautifully executed paintings of wild animals. The animal series is highly prized by Stick's fans.

To better understand the appeal of Stick's subjects, one must remember that in the early 1900s almost 90 percent of the American population lived outside large metropolitan cities. Surely, many could relate to the subject matter of hunting, fishing, and camping; all part of the rural way of life, and often a necessity for providing food. As the century progressed, the West was conquered, small towns became small cities, and many left their wilderness settings for more urban pursuits. Like the "dream girls" of other artists, Stick's rugged outdoor scenes would stir the romantic imaginations of many an urban businessman, clerk, and laborer whose chances for these rustic adventures would have to be saved for the occasional vacation.

The Open Season, ca. 1922

A Surprise Attack, ca. 1919

A Big Grizzly, ca. 1916

Untitled, ca. 1918

Their Christmas Dinner, ca. 1910

Breaking the Jam, ca. 1931

Untitled, ca. 1914

Racing the Storm, ca. 1912

The Catch of the Season, ca. 1918

The Home Trail, ca. 1926

The Big Prize, ca. 1916

The Lumberjack, ca. 1915

Untitled, ca. 1914

Untitled, ca. 1913

Surprised, ca. 1919

False Friends, ca. 1920

Untitled, ca. 1918

On Guard, ca. 1915

Hooked, ca. 1915

Hooked but Not Caught, ca. 1916

Untitled, ca. 1912

Untitled, ca. 1916

Quick Buddy, Shove Off, ca. 1924

Untitled, ca. 1918

Untitled, ca. 1925

The Covered Wagon, ca. 1918

Children of the Night, ca. 1918

Untitled, ca. 1923

Close Quarters, ca. 1920

Playing Him Out, ca. 1922

Hold On, ca. 1916

The Moose Call, ca. 1916

The Final Leap, ca. 1918

His First Pickerel, ca. 1922

Untitled, ca. 1916

Untitled, ca. 1918

Untitled, ca. 1923

Untitled, ca. 1921

Untitled, ca. 1919

A Pair of Hunters, ca. 1908

The Last Shot, ca. 1914

A Good Head, ca. 1915

A Kin to the Eagle, ca. 1913

Untitled, ca. 1922

The Thundering Herd, ca. 1911

By the Campfire's Ruddy Glow, ca. 1914

Untitled, ca. 1916

Shooting the Rapids, ca. 1914

Security and Trust, ca. 1918

Untitled, ca. 1920

In the Mist, ca. 1912

Untitled, ca. 1922

William McMurray Thompson
(1893-1967)

William Thompson's career can truly be called a Horatio Alger story. He eventually owned the art studio where he had started years earlier by sweeping floors! Born in Philadelphia, Thompson ran away from home at the age of thirteen and made his way north to New York. There he secured a job sweeping floors in the art studio of William Henry Chandler, a well-known artist of the time. Thompson soon displayed a curiosity and obvious propensity for art. He was further encouraged by Chandler, who taught him to draw and paint. Eventually Thompson pursued his academic studies at both the Art Students' League and the National Academy of Design in New York.

Once on his own in the commercial art field, Thompson soon made a name for himself. Primarily a landscape painter, his appealing works caught the attention of many of the art houses and calendar companies of the day. He consistently worked on commission basis for such firms as Louis F. Dow, Brown & Bigelow, Knave, and Gerlach-Barklow Company. With the outbreak of World War I, as his popularity was ascending, Thompson enlisted in the U.S. Army and served in the infantry in France. While fighting in the war, Thompson sustained eye injury from mustard gas, certainly a detrimental condition for any artist. With his eyesight damaged, but mostly intact, Thompson came home at the war's end. He returned to the Chandler studio and eventually bought the studio when Chandler retired during the 1920s.

Thompson resumed his career and maintained the studio until 1930. The stock market crash and the subsequent Great Depression forced Thompson to close his studio. He continued to work at home, but the demand for his style of illustration diminished as the 1930s progressed. In 1940, at the age of forty-six, Thompson took the position of Assistant Superintendent of the New Jersey Home of Disabled Veterans in Menlo Park. He was named Superintendent in 1946. Stricken with Parkinson's disease, he retired from the position in 1954. During his career as superintendent, during his retirement, and until his death in 1967 at sixty-four, he continued to paint in oils.

Unlike many of the popular calendar artists of his time, it appears that William Thompson did few, if any, illustrations for magazines or books. His work was almost exclusively landscapes, appearing mostly as framed art or on calendars. He can truly be called one of the most memorable and prolific artists in this popular field. His most recognizable subjects are, undoubtedly, the "cottage with flower garden" and "cabin in the woods by a lake" scenes. Exquisitely colored and softly textured, these scenes have a strong romantic and sentimental quality. Service in World War I gave Thompson, like many others, his first trip to Europe. One can easily discover European influences in his subject matter, particularly in the flower-strewn, thatched English cottages and gardens, rustic windmills, and Alpine-like mountains looming in the backgrounds of his scenes. More homegrown subjects include rustic mountain cabins by lakeside glades, fields at harvest time, and waterfalls.

Undeniably, one of Thompson's most appealing genres is his winter landscapes. With titles like "The Road to Home," "The Cheering Welcome Glows," and "Winter Moonlight," these scenes are highly evocative. Many are moonlit scenes and Thompson's use of color and light evoke the mood and feeling perfectly. Many calendars must have featured one of these snowy scenes for the December page. Like other pastel artists of the time who also made their own supplies, Thompson had greater control over his technique. Jo Ann Havens Wright, a Thompson enthusiast notes, that may explain ". . . the vivid Thompson blues and those brilliant orange sunsets we have all come to recognize as his." Thompson also painted a series of tropical landscapes resplendent with palm trees. One print, "Moonlight Ripples," even shows a ship in the bay, something unusual for a Thompson print.

Collectors who prefer romantic landscapes over pin-ups will undoubtedly like Thompson. His earlier, less vivid-colored landscapes and his California flower garden prints are already commanding higher prices. His other work is still quite affordable and many collectors find something compelling in the rustic landscape genre. There is no mistaking the original genius of William Thompson and the wonderful style he helped create.

My Old Kentucky Home, ca. 1914

How Dear to My Heart, ca. 1925

In Days Gone By, ca. 1920

Peaceful Valley, ca. 1925

In the Shock, ca. 1928

Snow Time, ca. 1935

Autumn Brilliance, ca. 1941

Moonlight Ripples, ca. 1929

Winter's Crimson Sunset, ca. 1940

The Road to Home, ca. 1940

Cozy Cabin, ca. 1935

Silent Winter Night, ca. 1938

Washington's Birthplace-Virginia, ca. 1928

Lake O'Hara, ca. 1930

Path of Blossoms, Hollywood, Calif., ca. 1935

Apple Blossom Time, ca. 1930

Untitled, ca. 1924

Moonbeam Reflections, ca. 1935

On the Wing, ca. 1944

Land of Dreams, Pasadena, Calif., ca. 1935

Ever Flowing, Ever Turning, ca. 1925

Grandeur of the Rockies, ca. 1930

A Cozy Cottage, ca. 1938

Rustic Home and Garden, ca. 1941

Great Outdoors, ca. 1923

Winter Camp, ca. 1945

Yosemite Falls, ca. 1935

Sunset Glow, ca. 1930

In the Land of Hearts Desire, ca. 1925

A Moonlight Melody, ca. 1936

A Cottage of Flowers, ca. 1931

Winter Splendor, ca. 1946

Winter Days, ca. 1920

Untitled, ca. 1926

The Cheering Welcome Glows, ca. 1928

Winter Moonlight, ca. 1939

Untitled, ca. 1920

Campfire, ca. 1935

Untitled, ca. 1925

Glories of the Rockies, ca. 1940

Moonlit Waters, ca. 1930

The Setting Sun, ca. 1920

Road to Home, ca. 1952

Snowbound, ca. 1936

Broken Solitude, ca. 1934

Wintery Night, ca. 1920

The Old Mill Stream,
ca. 1930

The Abandoned Mill, ca. 1925

Rocky Shore, ca. 1930

Tropical Moon, ca. 1940

When the Leaves Begin to Fall,
ca. 1930

'Twas the Night Before Christmas,
ca. 1937

Chester K. Van Nortwick

(1881-Date unknown)

C. K. Van Nortwick was an early art print and calendar illustrator whose work is receiving increased recognition. Despite this renewed interest, little is known of the artist's personal and creative history. It is known that he was born in Rhode Island and moved to Denver, Colorado, at an early age. After a number of years of study and private instructors, he entered the Art Institute of Chicago.

His work first appeared from the mid-1920s to the mid-1930s. Van Nortwick's work was published almost exclusively by the Gerlach-Barklow Company of Joliet, Illinois, which also held the copyrights; however, a small number of Van Nortwick's images were published in the 1920s by the Columbian Colortype Company in Chicago.

Gerlach-Barklow's publicity releases gave little personal information about Van Nortwick. They described him only as a "well-known painter of allegorical subjects, whose works suggest the quality of Maxfield Parrish." Indeed, Van Nortwick's earlier work seems to display many of Parrish's stock-in-trade images: urns, fountains, mountains, and languid beauties reposing in lush romantic landscapes. But Van Nortwick's landscapes had a decidedly country club setting. Van Nortwick women in these early pieces are not Parrish women; they sport a 1920s "flapper" look which is reflected in their hairstyles and the cut of their gossamer gowns.

Between 1927 and 1930 Van Nortwick painted three sets of twelve paintings intended as prints for monthly mailings. The sets were entitled "Mother Goose," "Fairy Tales," and "Boyhood Heroes." Like some of his earlier work, the Mother Goose and Fairy Tales series blatantly borrow from Parrish's trademark images and techniques: the deep blue skies and tumbling clouds; the highly stylized symmetrical compositions; and Parrish's classic characters and poses. In fact, The Golden Goose looks at first like a Parrish original. The paintings in the "Boyhood Heroes" series are more straight forward images of masculine subjects such as Sir Galahad, Robin Hood, and Rip Van Winkle,

painted in a style similar to the great illustrator of boyhood heroes, N. C. Wyeth.

This comparison should not suggest that Van Nortwick was not a competent and creative illustrator. When he broke free of imitative boundaries, Van Nortwick's work contained a distinctive beauty and charm. His forays into his own stylistic interpretations in "Mother Goose" and "Fairy Tales" are wonderful and his "Boyhood Heroes" show his artistic command.

Today, many collectors are beginning to seek out Van Nortwick's calendar prints. His relatively short career (less than fifteen years) make fewer pieces available. His appealing artwork and association with the Parrish school still send many collectors diligently searching for his works.

Humpty Dumpty, ca. 1927

Hey Diddle Diddle, ca. 1927

Tom Tom the Piper's Son, ca. 1927

Jack and Jill, ca. 1927

Little Bo-Peep, ca. 1927

Simple Simon, ca. 1927

Peter, Peter, Pumpkin Eater, ca. 1927

The Year's at the Spring, ca. 1933

The Magic of the Dawn, ca. 1927

In the Garden of Melody, ca. 1931

The Fountain of Youth, ca. 1933

An Enchanted Garden, ca. 1931

Once in a Lovely Garden, ca. 1929

By the Garden of Dreams, ca. 1929

Untitled, ca. 1933

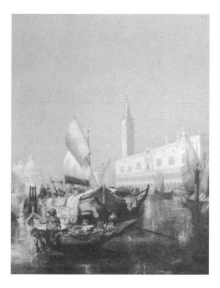

Venice the Golden, ca. 1932

Last of the Mohicans, ca. 1929

Rip Van Winkle, ca. 1929

Untitled, ca. 1926

Beautiful Gardens of Dreams, ca. 1931

The Dawn of Day, ca. 1930

The Grotto of Eternal Youth, ca. 1930

Tom Thumb, ca. 1930

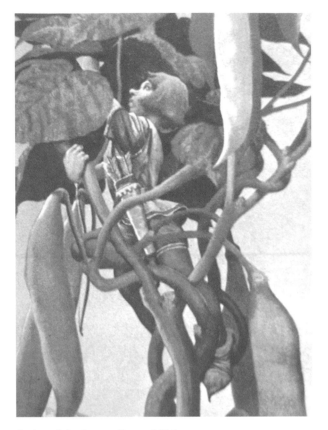

Jack and the Beanstalk, ca. 1930

Jack the Giant-Killer, ca. 1930

The Golden Goose, ca. 1930

Little Boy Blue, ca. 1927

Old Mother Goose, ca. 1927

Old Mother Hubbard, ca. 1927

The Ugly Duckling, ca. 1930

The Elves and the Shoemaker, ca. 1930

Captain Kidd, ca. 1929

William Tell, ca. 1929

Sir Galahad, ca. 1929

Robin Hood, ca. 1929

Just Fishin', ca. 1930

Hickory-Dickory Dock, ca. 1927

Hansel and Gretel, ca. 1930

Little Jack Horner, ca. 1927

The Sleeping Beauty, ca. 1930

Cinderella, ca. 1930

Robinson Crusoe, ca. 1929

Paul Revere, ca. 1929

Huckleberry, ca. 1929

Buffalo Bill, ca. 1929

Daniel Boone, ca. 1929

On Top of the World, ca. 1933

The Thanksgiving Turkey, ca. 1923

The Flying Trunk, ca. 1930

The King and the Golden Mountain, ca. 1930

Indian Maidens

Put a fringed dress, some beads, a headband, and feathers on a pin-up girl and you get an Indian maiden. A powerful image in the American psyche between 1910 and 1940, Indian maidens appeared everywhere in the graphic, art, and advertising worlds. They represent a last gasp attempt at romanticizing the closing of the Old West at the end of the nineteenth century. Indian maidens adorned almanacs, posters, sheet music, cigar boxes, and countless other products. By far one of the most widespread appearances was on calendars. Every major calendar company had a line of Indian maidens. They were used on calendars as small as ink blotters or as large as wall-size billboards. The most popular use was on monthly mailers. These were mailed out in sets of twelve, usually painted by the same artist, measuring four-by-six inches. The Indian maiden remained a familiar image until the 1940s. By then, more provocative pin-ups were gaining popularity. This standard image was discarded for more up-to-date fantasies.

In painting the Indian maidens, the dress and beadwork were as fictional as the Caucasian women who posed for the artists. Many artists, particularly in big cities, did not bother to study the small amount of information available at the time on Indian culture. Had they done so, they would have learned that each piece of clothing was symbolic and specific to each tribe. However, all authenticity would probably have been lost on a buying public who just demanded that the artists continue to create a maiden that was more beautiful than the last one. Early Indian maiden prints were often hand-colored, unpretentious portraits. By the 1930s, the Indian maiden had evolved into a version of the glamour girl popularized in pin-up art.

Various artists contributed to the Indian maiden genre. Each had their own interpretation: some concentrated on elaborate costuming while others depicted simply-garbed maidens in various poses. Background and atmosphere were all-important, and the more skilled maiden painters were also adept as landscape artists.

Artists already discussed in this book who contributed to the genre include L. Goddard, The Arthur Studios, Adelaide Hiebel, Zula Kenyon, and R. A. Fox. Other artists who contributed to this style include the following:

Edward Mason Eggleston
(1887-1941)

Born in Ashtabula, Ohio, Eggleston graduated from Columbus Art School in Columbus, Ohio, at the beginning of the 1900s. He continued his studies under noted artists such as Albert Fowley, Alice Schilly, and Harvey Dunn, the latter a former student of Howard Pyle, the pre-eminent illustrator of the time. Eggleston lived in New York for most of his life, where he pursued a successful career as a commercial artist and illustrator. He created the famous sleepy little boy holding a tire and candle, forever associated with the "Time to Retire" slogan for the Fisk Tire Company. Eggleston's Indian maidens often sport elaborate costumes and beadwork.

F. R. Harper
(1876-1948)

Born in Rock Island, Illinois, he arrived in Chicago at the turn of the century to study at the Art Institute of Chicago, like many other contemporary calendar artists. He continued his studies in Europe and returned to Chicago in 1908. Harper enjoyed a successful career as a fine artist. His works were exhibited in the Metropolitan Museum of Art in New York. His mainstay was commercial illustrations for advertising and paintings for calendars. Besides beautiful women, Harper painted patriotic and historical scenes. Harper's Indian maiden paintings are some of the most beautiful in terms of overall mood and technique.

Homer S. Nelson
(Date Unknown)

Homer Nelson was also a product of the Art Institute of Chicago. He advanced his studies under C. York in Denver, Colorado. Nelson traveled extensively to southwest America, Egypt, the South Seas, and Asia. He probably comes closer than most Indian maiden painters in depicting actual Indian dress and artifacts. This is evident in a series he painted titled "Indian Heroines." His vivid use of color and exquisite backgrounds reveal Nelson's enthusiasm for his work.

Charles M. Reylea
(1863-1932)

Born in Albany, New York, during the Civil War, Charles M. Reylea studied under the famous painter, Thomas Eakins, at the Pennsylvania Academy of Fine Arts in the late 1880s. He finished his studies in Paris and New York, where he finally settled. Reylea contributed many illustrations to major magazines such as Century and St. Nicholas. He also contributed numerous paintings to the calendar field with a wide variety of subjects, including over a dozen Indian maiden calendars. His style is expressive and vivid.

James Arthur, Firefly, ca. 1922

James Arthur, Untitled, ca. 1925

James Arthur, Myra, ca. 1922

James Arthur, Aurora, ca. 1922

Charles Relyea, Untitled, ca. 1931

Charles Relyea,
Absence Makes the Heart Grow Fonder, ca. 1932

F. R. Harper,
Ramona, ca. 1930

F. R. Harper,
Untitled, ca. 1934

F. R. Harper,
Wenonah, ca. 1932

Adelaide Hiebel,
The Signal Light, ca. 1928

Adelaide Hiebel,
Queen of the Wildwood, ca. 1929

Adelaide Hiebel,
In the Heart of the Lily, ca. 1931

Edward Eggleston,
Flaming Arrow, ca. 1934

Hy Hintermeister,
Winding Stream, ca. 1921

L. Goddard,
Untitled, ca. 1928

Dupre (R. A. Fox),
The Land of Sky Blue Waters, ca. 1926

Edward Eggleston,
Untitled, ca. 1935

Hy Hintermeister,
Miss Cherokee, ca. 1929

Edward Eggleston,
Flames of the Mesa, ca. 1936

R. Atkinson Fox,
In Meditation Fancy Free, ca. 1927

R. Atkinson Fox,
Daughter of the Setting Sun, ca. 1928

R. Atkinson Fox,
In Moonlight Blue, ca. 1931

Dupre (R. A. Fox),
Wanetah, ca. 1928

Dupre (R. A. Fox),
Ramona, ca. 1928

Deforest (R. A. Fox),
Pride of the Blue Ridge, ca. 1928

Hy Hintermeister,
Minnehaha, ca. 1926

F. R. Harper, Moonbeam Princess, ca. 1932

R. Atkinson Fox, White Feather, ca. 1930

Hy Hintermeister,
Laughing Maid, ca. 1921

Hy Hintermeister,
Makahwee, ca. 1921

Zula Kenyon,
The Land of Sky Blue Waters, ca. 1915

Zula Kenyon,
'Neath the Warm Southern Moon, ca. 1912

Zula Kenyon, Land of Laughing Water, ca. 1929

L. Goddard, Nawadaha, ca. 1928

L. Goddard, In the Valley of the Moon, ca. 1926

L. Goddard, Call of the Wild, ca. 1926

L. Goddard, Untitled, ca. 1926

Homer Nelson, Mountain Flower, ca. 1930

Homer Nelson,
The Dawn of Woman, ca. 1930

Homer Nelson,
Whispering Leaves, ca. 1930

Homer Nelson,
The Slender Maiden, ca. 1930

Homer Nelson,
Flat Arrow, ca. 1930

Homer Nelson,
The North Wind, ca. 1930

Homer Nelson,
The Blossom, ca. 1930

Homer Nelson,
Little Bird, ca. 1930

Homer Nelson,
Rising Sun, ca. 1930

R. Atkinson Fox,
Daughters of the Incas, ca. 1929

Adelaide Heibel,
The Heart of the Forest, ca. 1930

Adelaide Heibel,
Hiawatha's Honeymoon, ca. 1932

Fetterman,
The Song of the Waterfall, ca. 1929

Homer Nelson,
Yellow Bird, ca. 1930

Homer Nelson,
The Blue Bird, ca. 1930

Lippert,
Untitled, ca. 1930

Sultzer,
A Daughter of the Mountains, ca. 1926

(Artist Unknown),
Soreto, ca. 1932

L. Goddard,
The Land of His Fathers, ca. 1924

L. Goddard,
Untitled, ca. 1930

Hinton,
A Hasty Retreat, ca. 1938

Pricing Index

(Each entry in the Pricing Index contains the following: Title, measurement, value range, page number)

'Neath the Tropic Moon, 9x7, $35-$60, **85**
Oh What a Pal is Mother, 8x10, $25-$35, **88**
Out Where the West Begins, 7x10, $30-$45, **88**
Pandora 6x4, $15-$25, **86**
Pearl of India, 9x7, $35-$50, **91**
Penelope, 6x4, $15-$25, **92**
Playmates From Shadowland, 6x8, $25-$35, **84**
Spirit of Christmas, 12x9, $40-$65, **89**
Supper Time, 9x12, $25-$35, **88**
The Little Gray Home in the West, 9x7, $25-$35, **93**
The Love That Only Mothers Know, 12x9, $35-$50, **89**
Thiebe, 6x4, $15-$25, **86**
Untitled (couple and dog), 9x12, $25-$35, **93**
Untitled (family and cabin), 12x9, $25-$35, **93**
Untitled (family at home), 8x10, $25-$35, **84**
Untitled (family gathering), 10x8, $25-$35, **93**
Untitled (family on a picnic), 8x10, $25-$35, **88**
Untitled (woman and column),10x8, $35-$50, **85**
Untitled (woman by fountain), 10x6, $25-$45, **89**
Untitled (woman in grass skirt), 12x9, $40-$65, **85**
Untitled (woman on rock), 8x6, $30-$45, **86**
Untitled (woman with dog), 12x10, $40-$65, **93**
Untitled (woman with horse), 7x9, $50-$85, **92**
Untitled (woman with sword),10x7, $30-$45, **91**
Untitled (women with crystal ball), 8x6, $25-$35, **89**
Waiting for Daddy, 6x8, $25-$35, **88**
Waterlily, 10x8, $35-$50, **91**
Where Love Abides, 6x8, $25-$35, **84**

Phillip R. Goodwin

A Break at Dawn, 10x12, $35-$50, **96**
A Challenge, 8x11, $35-$50, **100**
A Chance Shot, 10x12, $35-$50, **95**
A Northwoods King, 8x10, $35-$45, **96**
A Prize Catch, 11x8, $35-$50, **103**
A Steady Hand at the Helm, 9x12, $45-$75, **99**
A Successful Call, 9x12, $45-$65, **96**
A Tense Moment, 9x12, $35-$60, **96**
A Thrilling Moment, 8x6, $30-$45, **99**
A Welcome Opportunity, 8x12, $45-$75, **96**
Admiring His Nerve, 9x12, $45-$65, **97**
An Early Morning Thrill, 10x8, $30-$50, **103**
Blazing the Trail, 9x12, $45-$65, **101**
Breaking the Jam, 9x12, $45-$75, **99**
Bruin Survivors, 8x10, $30-$45, **98**
Cruisers Making a Portage, 9x12, $45-$60, **101**
Forest Ranger, 9x12, $45-$65, **102**
Hewing the Way, 7x10, $35-$50, **101**
In God's Country, 6x9, $30-$50, **102**
In Strange Waters, 9x12, $45-$65, **100**
In Turbulent Waters, 8x10, $35-$60, **100**
Moose Hunting, 9x11, $45-$65, **96**
Nearing the End, 9x12, $35-$50, **102**
Out Where Skies Are Bluer, 8x12, $45-$75, **95**
Reel Sport, 5x8, $20-$35, **103**
Supper in Sight, 9x14, $50-$85, **103**
Surprised, 10x8, $35-$50, **95**
Taking the Trail, 8x6, $25-$35, **99**
The Cruisers, 9x12, $45-$60, **99**
The Dawn of a Perfect Day, 9x12, $35-$50, **95**
The End of the Day, 8x11, $40-$50, **100**
The Herder, 10x8, $35-$50, **101**
The Refugees, 9x12, $35-$50, **103**
The Right of Way, 8x12, $30-$40, **98**
Time for Action, 5x8, $25-$35, **102**

Unexpected Visitors, 5x3, $15-$25, **97**
Untitled (bear and cabin), 5x7, $30-$50, **97**
Untitled (bears and beehive), 10x12, $35-$50, **98**
Untitled (campers and forest fire), 8x11, $35-$50, **100**
Untitled (hunter and elk), 9x7, $35-$45, **95**
Untitled (hunters camping), 26x10, $125-$145, **94**
Untitled (man on horse), 6x9, $25-$35, **102**
Untitled (men fishing), 8x10, $35-$50, **102**
Untitled (men riding river logs), 7x10, $35-$50, **100**
Untitled (moose), 12x9, $35-$50, **97**
Untitled (mother bear with cubs), 9x12, $35-$50, **98**
We're Going Home, 9x12, $35-$50, **97**
When Action Counts, 6x8, $30-$45, **98**
Where the Tall Pines Grow, 9x12, $45-$60, **101**
Who's Coming, 9x12, $35-$50, **98**

Adelaide Hiebel

A Girl I Know, 9x7, $35-$45, **108**
A Maiden Fair, 13x10, $45-$65, **108**
An Old Sweetheart of Mine, 9x7, $35-$45, **109**
Be It Ever So Humble, 9x12, $15-$20, **115**
Bloom of Youth, 9x7, $35-$45, **108**
Cheerio!, 7x9, $35-50, **110**
Chums, 10x5, $50-75, **110**
Daydreams of Summer, 13x10, $30-$45, **113**
Family Portrait, 7x9, $20-$25, **114**
Friendly Little Fellows, 7x9, $20-$25, **115**
Guardian of Yosemite, 7x9, $15-$20, **115**
How Dear to My Heart, 13x10, $45-$65, **110**
I Should Worry, 9x7, $35-$45, **105**
I Wanna Be a Lindy, 7x9, $65-$85, **113**
In Dreamland, 9x7, $25-$35, **114**
Isabel, 9x7, $35-$45, **109**
Jessamine, 9x7, $35-$45, **108**
Love's Fairest Flower, 9x7, $35-$45, **112**
Me and My Pal, 9x7, $40-$50, **109**
Moonlight and Roses, 8x4, $45-$60, **111**
My Dixie Sweetheart, 14x11, $45-$65, **107**
Nature's Cathedral, 9x7, $15-$20, **115**
Outward Sunshine, Inward Joy, 7x9, $30-$35, **113**
Pals, 13x10, $50-$75, **110**
Phyllis, 9x7, $35-$50, **108**
Safety Sue, 5x4, $15-$25, **112**
Spanky's Safety School, 9x7, $35-$50, **112**
Stop!, Look!, Listen!, 9x7, $30-$35, **112**
Sunshine, 8x7, $30-$45, **111**
Sweet Baby O' Mine, 8x10, $30-$35, **104**
Sweet Girl of My Dreams, 9x7, $35-$45, **108**
Sweet Solitude, 6x8, $35-$45, **113**
Sweetheart of the Range, 9x7, $50-$85, **110**
The Bluebird's Garden, 14x10, $45-$65, **105**
The Bluebirds Are Here Again, 9x7, $35-$45, **112**
The Buckaroo, 13x10, $30-$35, **114**
The Gobble-uns'll Get You, 9x7, $30-$35, **105**
The Old Stone Bridge, 7x9, $15-$20, **115**
The Professor, 9x7, $25-$35, **106**
The Temptress, 9x7, $30-$45, **105**
The Traffic Cop, 9x7, $30-$35, **113**
This Little Pig Went to Market, 8x10, $30-$35, **114**
Those Endearing Young Charms, 13x10, $45-$65, **109**
Under the Southern Moon, 9x7, $35-$50, **109**
Untitled portrait (girl with dogs), 9x7, $35-$45, **109**
Untitled portrait (woman with dog), 12x9, $65-$85, **110**
Vacation Days, 9x7, $35-$50, **111**
Washington and His Birthplace, 15x10, $40-$50, **115**

About the Authors

Rick and Charlotte Martin have been avid calendar art collectors for nearly a decade. Their first love was the highly prolific works of R. Atkinson Fox. Through the years, the pursuit for Fox prints led the Martins to discover a myriad of other calendar artists, all who deserve recognition in their own right. With little information available to aid them in their search, their quest for knowledge became an authentic treasure hunt. And the more they uncovered, the greater their passion. This book is a first-time compilation of the forgotten calendar artists and the companies who made them famous. The Martins live in Columbus, Ohio, where they continue to pursue the art of the calendar.

Write for a complete catalog:

Collectors Press, Inc.
P.O. Box 230986
Portland, OR 97281